YOUTH PROSTITUTION IN THE NEW EUROPE

The Growth in Sex Work

Edited by
D. Barrett with E. Barrett
and N. Mullenger

Russell House Publishing

First published in 2000 by:
Russell House Publishing Ltd.
4 St. George's House
Uplyme Road
Lyme Regis
Dorset DT7 3LS

Tel: 01297-443948
Fax: 01297-442722
e-mail: help@russellhouse.co.uk

British Library Cataloguing-in-publication Data:
A catalogue record for this book is available from the British Library.

ISBN: 1-898924-61-9

Typeset by The Hallamshire Press Limited, Sheffield

Printed by Cromwell Press, Trowbridge

Russell House Publishing

Is a group of social work, probation, education and youth and community work practitioners and academics working in collaboration with a professional publishing team. Our aim is to work closely with the field to produce innovative and valuable materials to help managers, trainers, practitioners and students. We are keen to receive feedback on publications and new ideas for future projects.

Contents

Acknowledgements

'Are you looking for business?' is a question I am familiar with in relation to the subject matter of this book.

More importantly, does the book 'do the business'? Although biased, we think it does! Several elements of the book are unique and we hope it will lead to a well-known maxim changing from 'everybody's business is nobody's business' to 'nobody's business is everybody's business'. Ambitious, we know, but we are looking to change agendas and to have some impact.

Lots of friends, colleagues, relatives and organisations are worthy of mention. They know who they are, but I have taken the controversial liberty of identifying two only: the University of Luton, because they provided many forms of support, and Russell House Publishing, for similar reasons.

Lastly, many young people 'in the business' have given us their time, advice and help in order that this book be published. Thank you.

David Barrett
On behalf of the contributors

About the Contributors

David Barrett is Professor of Applied Social Studies, University of Luton.

Emma Barrett is studying Law and French.

Stewart B. Brodie is Senior Lecturer in Social Work at Robert Gordon University, Aberdeen.

Simon Brooke is co-ordinator of Social Policy Research and Development at Focus Ireland, Dublin.

Alyson Brown is a lecturer in Crime and Social History at the University of Luton.

Robert Buckley is Senior Lecturer in Social Work at Robert Gordon University, Aberdeen.

Penny Dean is a Regional Manager for The Children's Society.

Tim Lenihan is Head of Press and Media Relations at The Children's Society.

Nicola Mullenger is a freelance writer and photographer.

Doina Nistor is a lecturer in Social Work at the University Alexandra Ioan Cuza, Iasi, Romania.

Ambreen Shah is a Researcher in Social Policy at the University of Luton.

Svetlana Sidorenko-Stephenson is a Senior Lecturer in European Social Policy at the University of Luton.

Contiu Tiberiu Cristi Soitu is a lecturer in Psychology at the University Alexandra Ioan Cuza, Iasi, Romania.

Preface

Lynne Ravenscroft JP
Selborne, Hampshire

It is both profoundly important and profoundly depressing that this book about the abuse of children through prostitution across Europe is being published at the beginning of the second millennium. As anyone knows who has interviewed sex workers, it is essential that politicians and policy makers should understand what is happening in the lives of these, our fellow human beings. It is also desperately discouraging that vulnerable young people should still find themselves in this appalling situation, and that the level of exploitation should be increasing.

The various authors, whether academic researchers, political commentators, or members of charitable organisations working with vulnerable young people, describe the situation of sex workers across the geographical and economic spectrum of Europe, and particularly in the context of the break-up of the old Soviet Bloc. Liberation from Communism has meant the liberation from many kinds of censorship, with Budapest, for example, now being described as the centre of the European hardcore pornography industry. The relaxation of frontiers, the rapid advances in communication technology, and most especially the collapse of social security systems, have paved the way for a frightening increase in the trafficking of flesh, mostly of abused, homeless, or destitute young women.

It was in 1913 that Emily Pankhurst wrote 'when women are politically and economically strong they will not be purchasable for the base use of vice'.

In Britain in recent years there have been many reports of the growing international outrage at 'sex tourism' in Asia, paedophile rings throughout the Continent, and sexual abuse in children's homes. These have prompted voluntary and statutory agencies as diverse as The Children's Society and Barnardo's, the Association of Chief Police Officers (ACPO), the Association of Directors of Social Services (ADSS) and the Magistrates' Association to investigate what has been happening to young people and children on the streets in Britain, to see whether they are protected or further damaged under the law as it stands, and whether reforms of the law or its application are indicated. This book extends that investigation to Europe, and in doing so throws up some sharp contrasts in governmental and societal attitudes.

In 1991, the UK ratified the United Nations Convention on the Rights of the Child, which defines a child as a person under the age of 18. The Convention requires governments to protect children from all forms of sexual exploitation and sexual abuse, whether through prostitution, pornographic performances and materials, abduction, or the sale or traffic in children for any purpose; and to promote the physical and psychological recovery and social re-integration of child victims in an environment that fosters their health, self-respect and dignity. Despite this, in Hampshire in 1992 a 10-year-old girl was cautioned as 'a common prostitute', a legal definition of a particularly pejorative character.

In 1995, the UN Committee on the Rights of the Child reported on the progress the British Government had made in implementing the Convention. It welcomed the 1989 Children Act and the consultation paper *Working Together*, but recommended that urgent action should be taken to deal with the sexual exploitation of children, with more emphasis both on prevention and on strategies to promote recovery from neglect, sexual exploitation and abuse. This would also bring the UK more in line with the Council of Europe's statement that "these abuses have 'assumed new and alarming dimensions at national and international level', and that action needs to be taken ... through the prevention, detection and assistance by increasing resources to police and welfare agencies to locate, support and provide reintegration programmes for these children."

Unfortunately, however, when the issue of decriminalisation of soliciting for prostitution by under-18s was debated in the House of Lords on 17th March, 1998, Lord Williams of Mostyn, Home Office Minister, said it 'would create a new market—I am sorry to use that word, but that is what it is—in 16 and 17-year-olds who could legally solicit. There is a serious risk that it will put more, not fewer, girls at risk from pimps and exploitation.' This presupposes that the clients, the sexual abusers, now take a rational decision not to proposition children for sexual purposes; although the evidence is clearly to the contrary. The Metropolitan Police in London claim that there is a premium on 13 to 16-year-old girls who provide sexual services. Older women are dressing up in short tunics, wearing little cotton socks and putting their hair in bunches for 75 per cent of their clients. This approach also ignores the extremely damaging effect that societal attitudes have on the self-esteem of sex workers, when research everywhere indicates that it is largely abuse in their childhood that has driven them into sex work.

Under The Children Act (1989), local authorities have an overriding duty to safeguard and promote the welfare of children in need living in their area. In child protection procedures, intervention is required where 'significant harm' is found, and investigations must be instigated, if necessary through other agencies. There is also a duty to provide accommodation for young, single homeless people who are considered vulnerable. Further, if a police officer has reasonable cause to believe that a child would otherwise suffer significant harm, they may take that child into police protection and must then inform the local authority of that decision.

The above national and international conventions and statutes provide a framework of welfare provisions for dealing with children—persons under 18—who are caught up in sex work and whose welfare is at risk. If we are to protect our young people from a life of exposure to violence and coercion, we need to comply fully with the UN Convention on the Rights of the Child and accept the welfare approach. When young people are offered help and do not fear criminal prosecution they are much more likely to give the police information leading to the identification of perpetrators and the criminal networks, often international, of which they are part.

We are beginning to get a pretty clear picture of what is happening in Britain, and now, with this book, what is happening in the rest of Europe. Trafficking in women and children for the purpose of prostitution is one of the most lucrative businesses worldwide, and one that is directly profiting from the globalisation of the world economy. It seems indisputable that without the closest co-operation nationally and internationally between the relevant agencies, and the exchange of best legislative and executive practice, we will be abandoning the least privileged and most vulnerable people in our societies to a hideous fate. No one who has stood on the streets alongside prostitutes waiting for and returning from their clients, can be in any doubt of that. As one 21-year-old in Sheffield told me, 'I do not expect to be alive in a year's time'.

And what of the abusers? The clients, the racketeers, the owners of brothels, bars, 'massage parlours' and 'saunas', the traffickers, the sellers and consumers of pornography, the sex-tour operators? Now, even shareholders in Prudential and Standard Life are major investors in SFI Group, the biggest chain of lap-dancing clubs. All of them need to explain just why they think anyone has a right to rent, buy or coerce another person's body and use it as they wish. When will they have the common humanity to realise that person could be their sister, their daughter, or even their son?

Chapter 1

Introduction

David Barrett

Europe is a major object of popular concern both of anxiety and enthusiasm in our everyday lives, (Bailey, 1998). It is experiencing the forces of social change, particularly since the fall of Communism in 1989. Existing European structures, institutions and some organisations appear under considerable strain in an ever increasing globalisation. The 1998/9 Kosovan crisis is an example of such matters. The entity of Europe itself will doubtless continue to evolve and thus change.

This was the backdrop for me when travelling around Western Europe in the late 1980s when my journeying sparked the seed of an idea for this book. Already, my own research was indicating that the problem of young people's involvement in prostitution was likely to continue rising in the short term because of economic inequalities, easier cross-border movement, the growth of international crime syndicates and the lack of sophistication and co-ordination of intervention services.

Some years later, I have heard in person from many people, including young prostitutes, sometimes in their own country, like the Romanians and the Irish, or at conferences, like the Lithuanians and Belgians. Not all have contributed chapters, but the book is more about capturing the spirit of the problem of youth prostitution and sex work in Europe rather than an exhaustive country by country analysis. The contributions are more by way of metaphor than a problem unique to those countries included.

The aims of the book

The book is aimed firstly at decision makers, policy makers and practitioners who work in the fields of social welfare, justice and community medicine, including such professionals as social workers, child protection workers, health visitors, community nurses, sexual health workers and probation officers. And secondly, at students and libraries in the higher education sector who will be pursuing studies in these areas; some pure social science students are most likely to take an interest too.

The problems associated with young people involved in prostitution continue to escalate. The spread of the problem throughout Europe has brought cries of shock and disbelief from both the media and governments. Local, national and international responses remain uncoordinated, reactive, poorly identified and under resourced.

Senior members of key agencies, the academic community and policy commentators, have been brought together by the lead editor to explore the topic from their own perspectives. Two themes, recent political and economic changes, are to the fore, and the following question is regularly asked, 'why has this phenomenon taken hold?'

The book also presents new models of practice, identifies helpful initiatives and points to a future characterised by inter-agency working within the context of community safety and child protection.

More about youth prostitution

In recent years there has been considerable concern expressed about the problem of youth prostitution abroad. However, research (e.g. Melrose, Barrett and Brodie, 1999), has revealed that young peoples involvement with prostitution is also a significant problem in Britain. Many of these young people are currently being cautioned, prosecuted and criminalised, rather than protected, while the customers and pimps who control and abuse these children are seldom prosecuted as offenders.

Most informed people argue that the continued use of the Criminal Justice System to prosecute such young people, gives out the wrong message to those who are being abused and to the adults who abuse them. The UK falls short of its obligations to children under the 1989 Children Act, Council of Europe Recommendations and the 1989 UN Convention on the Rights of the Child. Our legislation protecting children regarding this issue is piecemeal and our understanding is not informing strategies to protect these vulnerable young people in the streets. Other European countries fail their young people similarly. However, now, most serious European literature on the subject argues that interventions concerning young people and prostitution should be based on protection and not criminal proceedings.

Most years, different parts of the media show not an uncommon interest in the plight of young people working as prostitutes; sex and youth are a powerful cocktail. However, it does on occasions allow for some of the debates on the subject to be brought into the public domain. These include issues such as homelessness, safe sex and benefit changes to be explored in a non-sensationalist way. It is not just debates about prostitution that change, prostitution itself changes. It is relatively recently that the implied notion of prostitutes as women and girls has shifted to include men and boys. However, a generally accepted ratio of four girls to one boy involved in prostitution is widely held, although there are regional variations.

One of the most recently adopted and widely used definitions when discussing youth prostitution, to identify the nature of the behaviour concerned (and it is only a behaviour, not a person), is 'the provision of sexual services in exchange for some form of payment, such as money, drink, drugs, other consumer goods or even a bed and a roof over one's head for a night', (Green, 1992). Sometimes, third parties are involved like pimps.

For the record, 'child' refers to those under 18 as defined by the 1989 Children Act and the UN. Youth/young person is commonly accepted as more difficult to define. Sometimes, and this book is no exception, 'child' and 'youth/young person' are used inter-changeably. The emphasis here though is on those in the mid to late teenage years—not those at pre-puberty. Many researchers and field workers prefer the term 'sex worker' as it is both general and non-pejorative and acknowledges that prostitution can be seen as a form of work. This approach serves to link prostitutes with others in the sex industry, for example, off-street workers like masseurs and escorts whose experiences will converge with those of 'prostitutes'. However, this term is most inappropriate in the context of the young because of the inverse power relationship between adults and young people, and its usage dismisses the exploitative nature of youth prostitution. The legal position regarding young people and prostitution is complex and is consequently dealt with in each individual contribution.

However, some of the debates regarding sex work need identifying. For those who wish to obtain more detail on a country by country basis of legal definitions, trends and issues regarding children, I refer you to Sandy Ruxton's invaluable *Children in Europe*, (1996). Continuing to evolve from European and worldwide sources are debates, focusing primarily on adult sex workers, that are either 'anti-violence' and even in some cases 'abolitionist', or 'pro-rights'. Trying to take account of the criticism generated by these two movements, 'anti-violence' and 'pro-rights', is complex. However, there exists common ground over exploitation and thus the 'anti-violence' (all forms of prostitution are sexual violence) and 'pro-rights' (the right to work as a prostitute under good legal and social conditions), do have some overlapping understanding. Although the debates were initiated often by feminist groups, they can be applied to all ages and groups of sex workers. Under-age sex workers are involved in breaking the law with perpetrators (sex offenders), but it is important to acknowledge that young sex workers experience considerable camaraderie with one another whilst simultaneously understanding the 'anti-violence' and 'pro-rights positions'.

Who is involved? Indicators showing the prevalence of youth prostitution are difficult to establish. Information tends to be fragmentary, being based primarily on voluntary agencies and localised research projects, (Barrett, 1995). Although some practitioners who work with young people involved in prostitution will say that most are poor, young white girls aged 15–16 with troubled backgrounds, used by middle-aged or older men, it is difficult to get an international or national picture to support such claims. Data can also be worryingly unreliable.

But what of the wider view? The title of the Council of Europe's report *Sexual Exploitation, Pornography and Prostitution of, and Trafficking in, Children and Young Persons*, from the Council of Europe in 1993, implies that prostitution involving the young is connected with other major areas of crime. The report makes many recommendations to its member states, including the involvement of mobile units of social workers in specialist field work. With regard to prevention, the report also suggests that particular attention should be paid to children in certain high-risk groups (e.g. emotionally damaged children from broken homes, runaways, drug users and 'street children'), who are easy prey for pimps or recruiting agents. It further suggests that there should be systematic and continuous control by the police and social services of places that are likely to attract young prostitutes and their clients, such as stations, airports, seaports and so on. The Council of Europe published a further work, *Street Children*, in 1994.

Beyond Europe, the United Nations, via UNICEF, sees young people and prostitution as a universal phenomenon. However, and the word is used advisedly here, 'child' prostitution continues to be big business in several countries that have ratified the 1989 UN Convention on the Rights of the Child, which expressly condemns sexual exploitation of minors, as did the subsequent 1992 UN Commission on Human Rights. However, during the summer of 1996, UNICEF, End Child Prostitution in Asian Tourism (ECPAT) and the NGO Group for the Convention on the Rights of the Child, held a World Congress against Commercial Sexual Exploitation of Children, in Stockholm. A thousand delegates attended from across the world. The purpose of the congress was to draw international attention to the problem of commercial sexual exploitation of children and to combat all forms of this exploitation in the specific contexts in which they occur. Consequently, writers have not been slow to publish on the topic in recent years, (e.g. Kempadoo and Doezema, 1998).

UNICEF is also currently raising major questions about some elements of European Union (EU) economic strategies and outcomes, particularly in relation to European Monetary Union (EMU). It is investigating whether or not indicators of child welfare in member states have been converging over the last 10–15 years. Is it the case that there has been recent macroeconomic convergence, for example, but the disparities in child welfare over the longer term are increasing? Or, are the member states who appear to 'fail' the Maastricht criteria for EMU membership, in fact countries where child welfare compares favourably with countries who have satisfied the criteria. A number of obvious indicators present themselves for consideration in the empirical analysis of convergence, including child poverty rates, teenage parenthood, youth unemployment and indicators of juvenile crime and justice. In short, the introduction of a single currency will remove the ability of member states to follow independent monetary policy. But, it is intended there will be compensating advantages for member states; will these be real or imagined and positive or negative for the needs of young people?

Monetary matters also influence the existence and future of welfare systems around the different European countries. The 'Old and the New' are compared and considered by Munday and Lane, (1998), and social changes are analysed by Bailey, (1998). Some more theoretically based considerations regarding welfare are explored by others, (e.g. George, 1998; Ferge, 1998) and intervention opportunities for those working with vulnerable young people are considered too, (e.g. Cooper *et al.,* 1995; Ruxton, 1996).

Of all the new evolving elements of concern regarding youth prostitution in Europe, probably the most disturbing is the increase in trafficking of young people, mainly girls, across borders and also within countries themselves. It appears to be increasingly common and out of control. The following case example demonstrates this phenomenon:

A 16 year old Lithuanian girl was deported in 1994 from Israel back to her home country on the grounds that she possessed a false passport. It transpired the girl had worked as a prostitute in a brothel. During her stay, which lasted three weeks, she served approximately 200 men that yielded 3,000 dollars. This girl is one of many young Baltic teenage girls who are drawn into sex trafficking in increasing numbers. The daily newspapers in all Baltic States contain many advertisements where young, beautiful girls are offered work abroad as dancers, bar-girls or in certain cases baby sitters. In reality, the work behind these advertisements, namely work as striptease dancers or prostitutes, is concealed. The girls become dependent upon a pimp who usually takes care of their travel documents so that they are unable to go home. In many instances, the girl is also subject to contractual debts in respect of her ticket which she must 'work' off. A considerable proportion of the girls who are drawn into prostitution in this manner are, like the Lithuanian girl in Israel, minors, but the full extent of this trafficking is unknown. According to the police in Vilnius, the trafficking is arranged so that following the recruitment of the girl she is supplied with a false passport indicating she is older. Some are only 15 years old. The girl is transported to Poland on a false passport, then disappears, and new intermediaries take over. The final destination may be a brothel in, for example, Germany or Israel. The price to the person who supplies the girl is between 3,000 and 5,000 dollars, (Karlen and Hagner, 1996).

Now to the following contributions. Chapter 2 provides us with an overview of the key political, economic and social events and trends which have occurred in Western and Central and Eastern Europe (CEE) since 1989; the subsequent chapters develop the information that is given here. The chapter assesses the different rates at which countries of the CEE have developed their movement towards political democracy and economic freedom and the consequential effects on Western Europe. It argues that the breakdown of centrally planned economies since the 1960s has seen an increase in the independence and dynamism of these previously suppressed countries. The destruction of the Berlin Wall in 1989 symbolised this movement, the significance of this act being felt the world over.

Brown and Shah suggest that political change in Europe since 1989 has been dominated and steered by the democratisation of the CEE. The majority of reform has been found in the post communist changes occurring in the countries of East-Central Europe. While these countries continue their self-development and economic improvement, the consolidation of this democracy is now a prime focus. Political development has in certain cases been determined by the strength of nationalism in countries of the CEE. The rate at which it occurs can also reflect the pre-existing political capital that existed in each region. Despite seeing an expansion of the EU during the 1990s, it has been solely within Western Europe. The establishment of both the single market in 1992 and the Maastricht Treaty both apply only to existing member states of the European Community.

The political disintegration of the Soviet Empire brought economic and social dislocation for the countries of the CEE. The absence of well-defined national strategies saw the need for fundamental adjustments to deal with the withdrawal of secure employment and state welfare in the post communist countries. There existed no experience of self-government in these countries and political unease caused further uncertainty. The hyperinflation of the late 1990s was the culminating event of the deepening economic problems suffered by the CEE and it became a fundamental obstacle to economic development. At the same time, Western Europe was experiencing deep economic recession. The breakdown of the Exchange Rate Mechanism in 1993 threatened further advance towards economic and monetary union in Western Europe and only fuelled Euro-scepticism in Britain.

In the final section, Brown and Shah concentrate on the key social effects resulting from the visibility and occurrence of youth prostitution in Europe. They argue that the ability to sustain the provision of welfare has been reduced by the relative economic slowdown and unemployment levels in Western Europe. An increase in the cost of welfare and the difficulties in addressing the significantly different welfare systems that have evolved in different regions further accentuate this problem. In the countries of the CEE, the problem is even greater due to the inexperience in dealing with welfare. In some countries, they argue, the levels of unemployment caused large-scale poverty and deprivation and as a result the black market blossomed, accompanied by criminal activity involving pornography and the drugs trade.

Chapter 3 gives an account of child prostitution in England, primarily identifying it as an age-old institution that was recognised early in the Victorian Era as a problem within society. It describes the situation today in England as regards to the law and tells of the problems associated with the 1959 Street Offences Act. Lenihan and Dean give us details of the work carried out by The Children's Society, National Children's Homes, (now NCH Action for Children), and Barnardos in the field of child prostitution. As a result of The Children's Society's *The Game's Up* Campaign, it has been called for children in prostitution to be treated as victims of abuse rather than be criminalised. Lenihan and Dean analyse the 1998 Draft Guidelines issued by the Home Office and the Department of Health on how to deal with children caught up in prostitution.

The chapter examines the ways that children become involved in prostitution, and often a complex tale of a past life emerges. The theory of prostitution as a survival strategy is looked at and the major role that drugs have to play. Also, the relationship between children in prostitution and children in care is investigated and the difficulties in exiting the profession.

Government policy is examined in this chapter to see if it is effective in reducing poverty and consequently reducing prostitution. Lenihan and Dean give us an account of the legal picture that, with regard to sexual offences in Britain today, is confused and is presently under government review.

Chapter 4 examines the relatively undiscovered problem of child prostitution in Ireland. Brooke begins by looking at the changes in Irish society. Despite a reputation as a poor, conservative country, recent developments within the country have made this stereotype inaccurate. There has been extraordinary economic growth during the last decade; however, although there is a general increase in prosperity, poverty is still an unfortunate feature of Irish society.

Brooke notes that Irish society has become steadily more liberal during recent years, with developments which would have been unthinkable until a few years ago. In 1978, contraception was legalised, but it was not until a referendum in 1992 that changed the constitution to allow information on abortion to be published. Abortion itself still remains illegal. Homosexuality was legalised in 1993 and in 1995 a referendum changed the constitution to allow for divorce. The Catholic Church, which has played such an important role in Irish society, has had its reputation seriously undermined after a series of scandals and convictions of priests for sexual abuse, over long periods of time. People are starting to follow an 'à la carte' Catholicism, choosing to accept only certain parts of the church's teaching, although this is much opposed by the Catholic Church.

Brooke then investigates the various issues involving children at risk in Irish society, for example poverty, homelessness, juvenile justice and educational disadvantage. He goes on to examine the existence of child prostitution in Ireland, which has only been acknowledged relatively recently. This recent 'discovery' of child prostitution has meant that there is a paucity of research. Furthermore, the secrecy of any sexual activity or abuse, especially with under age people, makes research difficult. Confidential information at agencies has also hindered research. Brooke mentions the work of Focus Ireland and Barnardos and details the problems they encountered with their work; he also identifies the figures that were collected. He then examines the ways into child prostitution. He shows the 'pathways into prostitution' which have been identified by the Eastern Health Board's Working Group.

Brooke continues by explaining the nature of child prostitution. He looks at the exchange of money or other goods for sex and examines the evidence of pimping. Next, he notes the health risks associated with prostitution and comments on the lack of information available about the punters.

In the third part of his work, Brooke looks at ways in which prostitution can be prevented and how the children already involved can be helped. He looks at the services already provided, including centre-based and out-reach services, and the staff training that is necessary in dealing with this difficult issue. Finally, he suggests a national strategy is needed to consolidate the work of the local agencies.

Nicola Mullenger in Chapter 5 examines the problem of youth sex work in Italy, with an emphasis on illegal immigration. The huge movement of persons commuting in and out of Italy have made the statistics regarding youth sex workers disputed and difficult to collate. Yet, one fact is agreed, that the figures are rising and the age is lowering. This chapter has concentrated on the new 'phenomena' of mass immigration to Italy from Central and Eastern European Countries and also the smaller numbers of youth from Africa and Asia. Italy has never before in its history seen this quantity of immigrants and does not have an established infrastructure to manage their arrival. Mullenger is quick to point out that not all immigrants are involved in prostitution, but the influx of illegal workers has limited employment possibilities and consequently increasing crime. The risk of prostitution has inevitably increased.

The chapter talks of the legislation controlling prostitution in Italy, mentioning the Merlin Law (1958), and analyses the more recent legislation for a visa which appears to be more favourable towards the sex workers. Mullenger identifies the provincial, national and European organisations that have been established to support the young people involved in prostitution and the programmes that are being provided around the country.

Chapter 6 examines young people and sex work in the Netherlands. The sex industry in the Netherlands is well established and embedded within the culture of the country. I am therefore encouraged to take a more reflective approach in contemplating the considerable amount of material available. The issues are perceived from both an internal and external standpoint and political, ideological and empirical material is explored. This chapter features more information about the 'boys' in the sex industry too, because the denial found in other European countries about this issue, is minimal in the Netherlands. Work from recent Dutch publications is included and considers developed and sophisticated harm reduction interventionist strategies and models of practice. Analysis of the liberal approach towards youth sex workers concludes the chapter.

Chapter 7 looks at youth prostitution in Romania. It begins with a political, economic and social history of Romania and from this, the context in which prostitution has developed, becomes apparent. The causes of prostitution are investigated; the importance of the economic context is stressed together with other factors that might encourage prostitution. Past and current legislation is included; prostitution is presently a criminal offence under Article 328 of The Romanian Criminal Code, but here Nistor and Soitu analyse the arguments for and against decriminalisation. The chapter includes a typology of both the prostitutes and the procurers in Romania. It also gives us empirical evidence regarding the number of street children and information as to their background and the present situation regarding juvenile prostitution. Finally, the chapter looks at how Romania has created an international market in the trade of prostitution.

Russia straddles the European border, and Chapter 8 looks at prostitution and young people in Russia. It begins with an historical overview that provides a context within which the problems surrounding prostitution can be placed. During Soviet times, prostitution was largely removed from the public view, so the reforms within the Russian society have brought with them the reality of the situation. Prostitution soon came to be associated as a social consequence of these reforms and the lack of economic stability only increased its growth. Furthermore, as a consequence of the collapse of welfare provision and the instability of employment, children of vulnerable working-class families were often forced on to the streets. As sex was their 'only saleable commodity', (cf. McLeod, 1982), these children were targeted and exploited by the sex industry.

In this chapter, Sidorenko-Stephenson analyses the changes that have occurred in prostitution in Russia. It looks at government legislation, public perceptions of prostitution and the changing profiles of the people involved. The nature of child prostitution is particularly focused on. The final part of the chapter discusses the practical responses to prostitution in Russia, including juvenile prostitution.

Chapter 9 looks at the problem of child prostitution in Scotland. The chapter investigates the reasons why the recognition of child prostitution has been slow to materialise. While in England the issue has received some attention, there has been very little written on the subject in Scotland. An outline is given of the Criminal Justice System in Scotland and the Scottish child care system, with particular reference to dealings with child prostitution. Buckley and Brodie, in their chapter, give an overview of Scottish legislation and analyses its application to child welfare and criminal justice. The reasons for entering into prostitution are included and also the profiles of those involved.

References

Bailey, J. (1998). *Social Europe*. Longman.

Barrett, D. (1995). 'Child Prostitution'. *Highlight*, Series No 135. National Children's Bureau.

Cooper, A. *et al.* (1995). *Positive Child Protection: A View From Abroad*. Lyme Regis: Russell House Publishing.

Council of Europe (1993). *Sexual Exploitation, Pornography and Prostitution of, and Trafficking in, Children and Young Adults*. Council of Europe.

Council of Europe (1994). *Street Children*. Council of Europe.

Ferge, Z. (1998). Women and Social Transformation in Central-Eastern Europe: The 'Old Left' and the 'New Right'. In Brunsdon, E., Dean, H. and Woods, R. (Eds.). *Social Policy Review*, 10: pp 217–336. The Social Policy Association.

George, V. (1998). The Consequences of Welfare Reform: How Conceptions of Social Rights are Changing. *Journal of Social Policy*, 27(1): pp 27–36.

Green, J. (1992). *It's No Game*. National Youth Agency.

Karlen, H., and Hayner, C. (1996). *Commercial Sexual Exploitation of Children in Some Eastern European Countries*. Bangkok: End Child Prostitution in Asian Tourism (ECPAT).

Kempadoo, K. and Doezema, J. (1998). *Global Sex Workers*. Routledge.

Melrose, M., Barrett, D. and Brodie, I. (1999). *One Way Street: Retrospectives on Childhood Prostitution*. The Children's Society.

Munday, B. and Lane, G. (1998). *The Old and the New: Changes in Social Care in Central and Eastern Europe*. European Institute of Social Services, University of Kent.

Ruxton, S. (1996). *Children in Europe*. London: NCH Action for Children.

Chapter 2

Reflections on a Changing Europe

Alyson Brown and Ambreen Shah

Capitalism is not the best way of running things. Indeed, as Churchill said of democracy, it is the worst system, except for all the others.
(Lech Walesa, cited in *The Guardian*, 8/3/99)

This chapter gives an overview of what are considered to be some of the key political, economic and social events and trends occurring in Western, Central and Eastern Europe, (CEE), since 1989. Another primary purpose is to provide a contextual beginning for analysis of the more specific and in-depth chapters that follow on the subject of youth prostitution in Europe. In this light, many aspects of the changes in Europe since 1989 will not be covered. Therefore, neither the complex of structures and institutions that exist within the establishment of the European Union, (EU), nor the extensive trade and finance agreements concluded within and between the states of CEE and the EU will be detailed here. Overall the aim is to assess the differential rates of development in CEE and the impact that the arduous journey towards democracy and the liberalisation of their economies has had on Western Europe. This is important because, as Bideleux states, (1996: p 225), CEE has had to make a triple transition 'from Communist dictatorship to pluralist democracy; from Centrally administered to market economies; and from Soviet imperial hegemony to fully independent national statehood'.

Before proceeding, it is necessary to clarify how the regions of Europe will be referred to throughout this chapter. In the main, conventional descriptions have been used regarding the geo-political divisions of Europe. Therefore, the chapter refers to Western Europe and Central and Eastern Europe, (CEE). CEE has been further divided into four regions, because a new regionalism has evolved in post Cold War Europe which divides states of 'similar constellations of political and economic patterns', (Miall, 1994: pp 1–2). The four regions are East Central Europe, the Balkans, the Baltics and the states of the former Soviet Union. East Central Europe is comprised of Hungary, Poland, the Czech Republic and Slovakia; the Balkans includes Albania, Bulgaria, Romania and the Republics of former Yugoslavia; the three Baltic states are Lithuania, Latvia and Estonia, and finally there are the European states of the former Soviet Union, consisting of fifteen independent states, including the Ukraine and Moldova.

The reforms introduced by Mikhail Gorbachev during the mid 1980s were a crucial prelude to the breakdown of the Soviet empire. The implications of *glasnost* and *perestroika* were an open recognition that the Soviet State and its sphere of influence were experiencing severe economic problems and that political reform was needed. Fault lines had been appearing in the centrally planned economies since the 1960s and reforms attempting to address these had largely failed. The more open form of government, which resulted from the reforms, released previously suppressed opposition forces and enabled the expansion and legitimisation of diverse groups promoting civil rights, ethnic identity and environmental protection. In November, 1989, the power of these groups was symbolised, for the West, by the physical breaking down of the Berlin Wall. This has not only had a defining impact upon CEE, but has also had a far-reaching influence on world politics and in particular Western Europe.

Political Changes Since 1989

An important priority for the whole region of CEE has been to engage in a process of democratisation. The countries of East-Central Europe comprised the leading edge of reformism since 1989 and have since remained at the forefront of post-communist change. For instance, Poland was the first country to establish a non-communist government which was led by Lech Walesa and commanded a considerable popular following. In the West, Walesa was portrayed in the media as a heroic figure who, through the Solidarity Trade Union movement, sparked the breakdown of Communism and later prevented neo-communists from returning to power. Therefore, although the conflict and major uncertainties experienced in this region have received extensive coverage in the Western media, it cannot be denied that a broad framework of constitutional and democratic order in which extensive civic freedoms, a relatively well-functioning legal system and largely free press have been established. The focus now for these countries is how this democracy can be consolidated, even if this is of 'an imperfect variety' and some way from the model of West European pluralist democracy, (Lewis, 1998: p 26). Hungary, Poland, the

Czech Republic and in particular Slovakia, suffer from problems of 'elitism, rather weak party systems, poorly developed civil societies and often having dubious links with the freewheeling practices of a rapidly developing free market capitalism', (Lewis, 1998: p 25). These problems have not been insurmountable in the drive for political reform and economic recovery in East-Central Europe, but the same cannot be said for the countries in the Balkans and the European states of the former Soviet Union.

Gallagher gives three ways in which civic freedoms and free elections were abused in these other regions. He states that corruption occurred in securing and augmenting political power as well as in managing political competition, (Gallagher, 1998). In Serbia and Romania, for instance, processes for free elections were undermined by former communists putting forward a plethora of different parties to confuse the electorate and make it difficult for their centre-right opponents to be promoted as a real alternative. In Romania, between February 1987 and September 1991, President Illiescu used coalminers to disperse his anti-communist opponents and then to drive his own prime minister from power following a quarrel over the pace of political reform. Finally, in Albania, Serbia and Croatia during the first half of the 1990s, the media was put under pressure, the judiciary prevented from defending citizen's rights and the secret police were an increasingly autonomous force. The motivation for such activities was a reluctance to allow the wealth accumulation of the government and their allies to be scrutinised, as in many countries large numbers of ex-*nomenklatura* diverted state resources into their own hands through bogus efforts at privatisation, (Gallagher, 1998: pp 47–50).

In Hungary and Poland, members of the ruling elite began to transform state assets into personal private property before the collapse of the Soviet Empire. In this light, the return to power of former communist leaders post-1989 in Hungary and Poland cannot be seen as a direct political turn around consequent on economic disillusionment, but as setting the political seal to processes already in motion, (Lewis, 1998: p 41). In contrast, in the Ukraine, Moldova and the Baltic Republic, (with the exception of Latvia), the return to power of ex-communist rulers between 1992–1998 was, according to Birch, because 'it became obvious that freedom from the Soviet yoke would not of itself solve the countries' economic problems', (1998: p 71). (See also Lewis, 1998: pp 40–42.) However, analysts have noted that the former communists that have returned to power everywhere in CEE, with the exception of the Czech Republic, have not been able to entrench their political power, (Taras, 1998: p 124). One consequence of such unstable leadership has been the manipulation of nationalist feeling.

To varying degrees, Nationalism has been used to mobilise political support, often by former communists and people who perceived Western-style modernisation as a threat. It has also frequently been employed to deflect criticism from the inadequacies of ruling parties. Although Nationalism has been an element in politics in East Central Europe, relative to the Balkans, its force has been limited. In Serbia, Nationalism has been an overt strategy in the political game. Radical Nationalism was inherent in Milosevics' ambitions for a 'Greater Serbia' and has fuelled conflict in the region throughout the 1990s. At the extreme, this has culminated in long-running hostilities in the states of the former Yugoslavia and the waging of war by NATO forces against Milosevic in Serbia. By June 1999 a tenuous peace was achieved in Kosovo, but some have predicted that, 'Over the next few months Kosovo is bound to be rocked by one crisis after another' and have warned that conflict could re-emerge in the neighbouring countries of Macedonia and Croatia, (*The Guardian* 15/6/1999).

The diversity of the political development reflected above is due in large part to the varying degrees of pre-existing political capital that existed in each region. Although there is no long-standing democratic infrastructure and legitimacy of such rule in most of the post-communist states, countries close to Western European borders came under Soviet influence later (during the 1940s) and have retained stronger cultural similarities with the West. According to Millard, the communists in Poland, for instance, never succeeded in establishing the legitimacy of single party rule or eradicating traditional anti-Russian and anti-Soviet attitudes. Moreover, the Polish population had widespread access, throughout the communist period, to external Western radio broadcasts and foreign travel, whilst also retaining strong family ties abroad, (1996: p 206).

In the West, the immediate impact of the breakdown of the Soviet Union, rather than being internal restructuring as was the case in CEE, was to provide an impetus to strengthen integrationist policies within the EU. According to Miall, the potential strength of Germany following re-unification, stimulated efforts to consolidate the European community, (1994: p 10). Establishment of the single market in 1992 referred only to existing member states, as to a great extent did the Maastricht Treaty. The Maastricht Treaty contained provision for political and monetary union. As Carr and Cope point out, its aim was to be an 'integrationalist blueprint that envisaged further deepening and widening of the European Community', (1994: p 67). Proposals included the Social Chapter, the transfer of additional responsibilities to the European Union (EU) and the movement towards a common foreign policy. However, the expansion of the EU during the 1990s has been solely within Western Europe, with the primary objective of internal consolidation and co-operation.

The priority given to internal consolidation was also reflected in the creation of 'Schengenland' in March, 1995. Under this agreement, the intention was to abolish internal borders. At the time, concerns were expressed by right-wing groups that any weak links in the external borders of states would allow large-scale immigration from CEE and North Africa. In fact, fears of immigration, along with a reaction to recession and resistance towards the EU and to the potential widening of its membership, have encouraged increased right-wing Nationalism in the West. The continuing prominence of immigration as a party political issue and the strengthening of external border controls has led to accusations of the establishment of a 'Fortress Europe', (Cesarani and Fulbrook, 1996: pp 3–4).

In the broader context, the defensive force in Western Europe, set up in 1949, is inextricably tied to the US, in the form of the North Atlantic Treaty Organisation (NATO). Conceived and matured in the Cold War era, its purpose and role during the 1990s was less explicit. As William *et al.* states, 'Preserving an alliance without an enemy and a strategy without a threat will not be easy', (Cited in Lawrence, 1996: p 56). Nevertheless, it can be argued that NATO has been given a renewed purpose with recent events unfolding in Kosovo. Whether this can be perceived as the humanitarian defence of European peoples, as has been popularly accepted, or in the extreme as the use of NATO as an imperialist instrument, only history will show.

Economic Changes Since 1989

For the countries in CEE, the political disintegration of the Soviet Empire was accompanied by economic and social dislocation. The breakdown exacerbated pre-existing problems produced by the stagnating economies, decaying infrastructures and the sometimes severe environmental problems. As Bideleux has pointed out, up to half of the industrial capacity inherited from the communist regimes was either 'technologically obsolete, environmentally hazardous or produced goods for which there was no longer a demand', (1996: p 229). In the years immediately following the collapse of the former Soviet Empire and Comecon, (council of mutual economic assistance) trade, industrial output plunged and inflation rates increased, often rapidly. Unemployment rates in almost all countries soared (with the exception of the Czech Republic), although not to the same extent, which implies that the over-manning practised under Soviet central planning often persisted. Certainly, it has been suggested that the number of 'post communists' that were returned in elections in CEE during the early 1990s was not, in this economic context, surprising, (Blazyca, 1998: p 207).

In the decade since 1989, the people of CEE have had to make some fundamental adjustments and face uncertainties that they have never faced on a wide scale before. Foremost among these have been the withdrawal of secure employment and state welfare in a context of new entrepreneurial economies and new distributions of wealth, influence and status, (Miall, 1994). Economically, the former German Democratic Republic was the most fortunate, already the most developed of the CEE States, it benefited in the longer term by its re-unification with West Germany. Nevertheless, East Germany experienced a decline in total jobs from 3.2 million to 1.3 million between 1989 and 1993 and a 45 per cent drop in GDP between 1989 and 1991, (Bideleux, 1996: p 229). Similar dramatic economic dislocations occurred throughout CEE during the first half of the 1990s. A UNICEF report released in 1994 concluded that by 1993 conditions were worse in CEE than those in Latin America during the 1980s or in Western Europe during the 1930s Depression, (Bideleux, 1996: p 228).

Many of these social problems continued in the absence of well-defined national strategies or policies, strong trade unions and the shortages of experienced and capable bureaucrats and managers, (Dobrinsky 1996: pp 389–390). Most of the states of CEE had no recent experience of self government and little institutional basis for national welfare provision. Furthermore, in many states the existence of disputed territorial boundaries and an often heterogeneous mix of ethnic minorities meant that there was no widely shared cultural identity, but fertile ground for nationalist extremism. Popular political unease and the widening poverty gap further ignited such nationalism, especially in the Balkans and Slovakia. Contemporaries were well aware of the dangers. Hungary's Foreign Minister Geza Jeszensky stated in 1993 that, 'This social environment creates space for the demagoguery of onetime Communists now donning national colours, as well as for the resurgence of extremist tendencies', (Bideleux, 1996: p 229).

By the mid 1990s recovery was underway in some countries of East Central Europe, namely Poland, Hungary and the Czech Republic, but many others, especially the former Soviet States, were experiencing deepening economic problems. By 1995, the GDP of the Czech Republic, Poland, Hungary and Slovakia had attained 85, 99, 86 and 84 per cent respectively of its 1990 level. In comparison, the similar figures for the Ukraine, Lithuania and Moldova were 46, 40 and 38 per cent, (European Bank for Reconstruction and

Development cited in Blazyca, 1998: p 213). In the Czech Republic, Poland and Hungary, the proportion of GDP achieved by the private sector had reached 70, 60 and 60 per cent respectively in the mid 1990s, whereas for the Ukraine, Lithuania and Moldova, these percentages were only 35, 55 and 30 respectively, (European Bank for Reconstruction and Development cited in Healey, 1996: p 6). It should be noted that this is not a private sector in the Western European sense. In many cases the ownership structures were not clear and the state retained a strong institutional influence, for example through banking and finance, (Blazyca, 1998: p 209). By the later 1990s, hyperinflation in many of the Eastern European countries, (that is all of CEE except the East-Central European states), especially those that were formerly part of Russia, proved to be a fundamental obstacle to economic development, (Blazyca, 1998: p 197).

The inherent advantages of the East Central European States over those further eastwards, were becoming increasingly evident in the differing rates of economic restructuring and growth. The continued existence of large state-owned enterprises and the low degree of change in the way they are operated has been cited as a major factor in the various rates of economic transition, (Dobrinsky, 1996). There is evidence of some adjustment and improved performance in these industries, but generally the large state-owned enterprises have been particularly resistant to restructuring and have been described as 'financial black holes', equipped with obsolete physical capital and heavily over-staffed, (Dobrinsky, 1996: p 393). Other writers have been more optimistic, although regionally specific about the level of change that has occurred. Blazyca gives three reasons why he believes state-owned enterprises in Poland, Hungary and the Czech Republic have 'often adapted remarkably well to new conditions'.

> *First, it was impossible even for* nomenklatura *managers to ignore the fundamental change in political climate. Second, alongside this, enthusiasm for privatisation meant that even in state firms, managers operated under a new threat and opportunity (for self-enrichment). Third, new economic policies tended to work well in countries like Poland, the Czech Republic and Hungary where a basic credibility in government policy existed*

(Blazyca, 1998: p 204).

For those countries in which these giant state-owned industries have continued to be a burden, their closure is very difficult due to their economic and political importance and the potential social consequences of increasing unemployment in this way. Yet they comprise a significant hindrance to economic modernisation and have continually to be bailed out financially. The wider effects of the continuance of these giants are evident. The produce of these industries, for example energy generation, remains centrally controlled, which distorts relative prices and affects allocative efficiency. Furthermore, by being so heavily over-staffed they distort the labour market and often maintain strong trade unionism with an inherent interest in the continuance of the old system. Within the difficult financial climate of transition, the consequences of the possible crowding-out of limited investment resources for the private sector by this large public sector must also be considered, (Dobrinsky, 1996: pp 394–396).

Generally, like political change, a diverse pattern of economic growth can be discerned in the development of the states of CEE during the 1990s. What has been described as East-Central Europe, has experienced 'the best performance in the region, with the shortest recessions, lowest inflation and fastest economic growth', (Blazyca, 1998: p 201). The European post-Soviet economies have experienced the poorest rates of growth and the greatest transitional difficulties, while the Baltics and Southern Europe reveal a gener-ally intermediate picture, (Blazyca, 1998: p 201). On the whole, those countries which had made the most progress towards economic transformation were those invited, in July 1997, to begin negotiating for future possible membership of the European Union, that is the Czech Republic, Poland, Hungary, Slovenia and Estonia, (Blazyca, 1998: p 210).

At roughly the same time as CEE was suffering the worst dislocating effects of economic transition, Western Europe was experiencing deep economic recession. Recession in Western Europe was in part a consequence of strains of the economic reunification of Germany and the uncertainty caused by the varying commitment shown to European Union under the Maastricht Treaty. Britain chose to opt out and Denmark narrowly voted to reject ratification of the Treaty. The culmination of such problems was the breakdown of the Exchange Rate Mechanism, most spectacularly in 1993. This event in turn threatened the further advance toward economic and monetary union in Western Europe. The variety of commitments to political and monetary union remains. Britain, for instance, has remained outside the single currency adopted early in 1999. Scepticism in Britain with regard to the single currency and 'Euroland' in general, was revealed by the strong showing of anti-European feeling in the European Elections of June 1999, which gave the Conservatives the largest number of electoral representatives by campaigning on the slogan 'in Europe, not run by Europe'. Elsewhere, the single currency has been viewed with much greater optimism. The Prime Minister of Portugal, for instance, stated in late 1998 that 'The Euro will be a fundamental instrument for the deepening of the

European Union, creating conditions for a larger political cohesion which will allow for a larger international role of the EU', (Guterres, 1998: p 153).

As stated earlier, a widening of the EU has not yet occurred beyond Western Europe. This has been partly due to the harsh economic climate of the early to mid 1990s. Many member states felt that the EU was not strong or stable enough to hold up under the additional pressures of a further widening to the East. The inclusion of states with the economic and political problems exhibited in CEE might exacerbate existing problems regarding social and regional funds, the Common Agricultural Policy and above all pose a threat to EU trade. In addition, it was asserted that the integration of CEE states into the EU would enable the migration of large numbers of their impoverished populations to look for work in Western Europe, where unemployment rates were already considered to be high, (10.8 per cent in 1996. Jackman, 1998: p 61), but where welfare provision was significantly better.

The broader context for the economic problems faced by Western Europe is the globalisation of the world economy which continues apace. Globalisation has been driven by a volatile combination of forces, including the 'strategies and practices of trans-national corporations and the dynamics of technological developments', (Dickens and Oberg, 1996: p 101). This has resulted in the speeding up of change in the industrial and financial markets and in the intensification of competition. Indeed, economic globalisation has been cited as the EU's greatest challenge and unemployment, its greatest problem, (Guterres, 1998: p 155). Certainly, the slow down in economic growth has in part been due to a loss of trade in one of Western Europe's most important export sectors—manufactured goods. Between 1980 and 1992, Western Europe's share of world manufacturing exports fell from 22 per cent to 18 per cent. In the traditional industries, ground was lost to the newly industrialised countries of South-east Asia, while trade in high tech industrial goods was lost largely to Japan. During the 1990s, industrial decline in Europe continued with Britain suffering the most, following extensive restructuring and modernisation, while industry in the former West Germany re-established a strong competitive position, (Lane, 1998: p 42).

A growing element of globalisation has been direct foreign investment. In Western Europe such investment has been heavily concentrated in Britain, Germany, France and the Netherlands. The major players outside Europe have been Japan and the US. Globalisation and the extension of massive multi-national corporations over the US, Western Europe and Japan has tended to direct attention away from CEE, which attracts a relatively small proportion of such badly needed investment.

Social Changes Since 1989

The political and economic changes outlined above set the context in which social conditions have been determined over the last decade. However, it is recognised that political, economic and social changes are inextricably linked and combine, over time, to produce fluid and dynamic processes of development. The aim here, therefore, is to concentrate upon some key social effects that may have resulted in the increased visibility and occurrence of youth prostitution in Europe.

The relative economic slowdown experienced by Western Europe and relative high unemployment has affected the region's ability to sustain previous levels of welfare provision. This has posed some difficult problems for the predominantly leftist governments during this period, particularly the choice between economic efficiency and welfare equalities. The cost of welfare has risen due to a number of factors including demographic change, rising cost of health care and the changing nature of the labour market. As Rhodes states, women have been particular affected:

> *The growing proportion of non-standard forms of work and the increasing workforce participation of women both challenge traditional arrangements—the first because such workers may be denied access to entitlements devised for permanent, full-time employees; the second because social protection is generally geared to male breadwinners and tends to penalise female careers.*
>
> (Rhodes, 1998: p 48).

The significantly different welfare systems that have evolved in the nation states of Western Europe, has led some to believe that a comprehensive common response to these problems is rendered impossible. Responsibility for welfare, in the main, continues to lie with individual sovereign states. However, the EU has been active in setting a minimum floor below which entitlements cannot fall, (Rhodes, 1998: p 48). Nevertheless, it has been argued that one strategy that can be discerned from welfare reform in continental Europe is that 'the price of adjustment should be shouldered by the unemployed, comprised largely of younger, female, and older workers', (cited in Rhodes, 1998: p 49).

Central and Eastern European countries, in the context of them having suffered greater political and economic problems, have experienced more profound social difficulties whilst having less financial resources to address them. Blazyca has pointed out that although there has been relatively little research on the pattern of income distribution, it is clear that regional differentiation and inequalities have sharply increased, (1998: p 208). A small group of people have been able to take advantage of the opportunities offered by marketisation. These have been identified as those using their entrepreneurial skills in newly formed businesses, those 'able to transform their control of former state property into newly privatised forms', and those who have transformed illegal earnings into legal forms of wealth, (Cox, 1998: p 228). Nevertheless, the fact remains that, as yet, there seems to have been less winners than losers.

Under Soviet collectivist rule, two basic benefits, which maintained standards of living, were guaranteed—the right to full employment and consumer price subsidies including rent and food. Within a centrally controlled paternalist state, social problems such as poverty, homelessness and crime were defined as non-existent. Benefits were seen as 'gifts rather than rights', (Munday, 1998: pp 5–9). Post-1989 political transformation and macro-economic considerations took priority and old systems of welfare provision, although deteriorating, often persisted. Of all the social problems experienced, unemployment was perhaps the most unprecedented and shocking for the population at the time. Between 1990 and 1994, all CEE experienced falls in the level of employment. One of the worst affected was Bulgaria in which employment dropped by 25.7 per cent, (cited in Cox, 1998: p 223). A major effect of this was large-scale poverty and deprivation throughout the region. Staying with Bulgaria, United Nations' estimates suggest that in 1992 over 50 per cent of Bulgars were in poverty, (cited in Munday, 1998: p 11). These high levels of unemployment encouraged the expansion of the shadow and black economies that have, according to Cox, mushroomed throughout most of the CEE states. Poverty has also encouraged criminal activity. A recent article in *The Guardian* suggests, for example, that the problem has become acute and that 'Drug trafficking and gangsterism are a key feature of the new societies'. The article also asserts that through the door opened by increased liberalisation, came the pornography and drugs trade from Western Europe.

> *Exiting have been an estimated 10,000 young women, many of them Romas and Gypsies, to work as prostitutes. They are probably the most dramatic illustration of the sexual exploitation of Eastern Europe, whether of Czech prostitutes in towns that border Germany or under-age boys in gay porn videos made in Prague.*
>
> (*The Guardian*, March 10th, 1999).

Women and young children have been amongst the most vulnerable sectors of the population in CEE along with the unskilled, single parents and the old. The position of women, for instance, has worsened considerably compared with the Communist era. Not only has social legislation protecting women been reduced over time, but they have been disproportionately affected by rising unemployment. In many countries, women have been the first to be made redundant as a result of the restructuring of labour forces. In the Czech Republic for example, the proportion of women of the total unemployed, between 1990 and 1994, rose from 50.9 per cent to 60.5 per cent, (cited in Corrin, 1998: p 238). With the withdrawal of workplace childcare provision, this situation is likely to get worse before it gets better. Although there has been a growth in the voluntary welfare sector, it has been suggested that unless the state takes a more active and structured approach the gap in social provision will widen, (Munday, 1998: p 15).

In general, increased unemployment and poverty can be taken as the main culprits when seeking explanations for increased family breakdown, alcoholism and rises in death and attempted suicide rates. As in the West, children often bear the brunt of such social conditions, (see Munday, 1998).

Conclusion

The political, economic and social developments since 1989 have served to confirm the shape of new regionalism. Western Europe, despite experiencing economic recession and the challenge of globalisation, has in fact maintained its political and economic standing in the world. It has been able to consolidate its power in Europe through the strengthening of the EU under the Maastricht Treaty and the establishment of the single market, and in the Western world partly through its close ties with NATO. CEE has not faired so well. East Central Europe has composed the leading edge of successful economic transition, yet by the mid 1990s only Poland had reached the levels of output that it had in 1989, with the other states in the region following closely behind. The political systems in this region achieved democratic consolidation some eight or so years into their new existence holding free elections, respecting civic freedoms and allowing a largely independent press. With regard to the Balkans, the States of the former Yugoslavia have dominated debate. The existence of heterogeneous and sizeable minority populations and nationalist leaders has combined to bring about large-scale conflict and devastation to the region. This has recently been illustrated by the events unfolding in Kosovo. Such conflict has crippled the physical infrastructure and general economic stability of the area. The Baltics and the states of the former Soviet Union have made significant political and economic progress, but in general, Post Soviet States have suffered the greatest transitional problems and achieved the poorest rates of growth.

Overall, unemployment and the poverty associated with it have, not surprisingly, dominated literature on the social conditions in CEE during the last ten years. Unemployment has also figured prominently in discussions of social change in Western Europe during this period. However, the better established systems of welfare provision, despite rising demand and increasing financial costs, have been better able to deal with these problems. The populations of CEE have not only experienced the deterioration of the security of full employment and subsidies on rent and food, but the low priority given to social welfare in the drive for political and economic reform has resulted in a widening gap between voluntary and state welfare services. The hardships suffered have undeniably been great, although it is questionable what alternatives are available.

The political influence of the US and Western Europe has produced a dominant ideology which dictates that capitalism, democracy and the free market are the only answers to economic development. Despite the pains of transition which have been suffered and continue to be suffered in CEE, this is still largely seen as the only way forward. To reiterate Lech Walesa's sentiment at the beginning of this chapter, this suggests an acceptance of the dictum that capitalism may be the worst system, except for all the others.

References

Alum, P. (1995). *State and Society in Western Europe*. Cambridge: Polity Press.

Bideleux, R. (1996). Introduction: European Integration and Disintegration. In Bideleux, R., and Taylor, R. (Eds.). *European Integration amd Disintegration, East and West*. London: Routledge.

Bideleux, R., and Jeffries, I. (1997). *A History of Eastern Europe: Crisis and Change*. London: Routledge.

Birch, S. (1998). In the Shadow of Moscow: Ukraine, Moldova, and the Baltic Republics. In White, S., Batt, J., and Lewis, P.G. (Eds.). *Developments in Central and East European Politics*. Basingstoke: Macmillan.

Blazyca, G. (1998). The Politics of Economic Transformation. In White, S., Batt, J., and Lewis, P.G. (Eds.). *Developments in Central and East European Politics*. Basingstoke: Macmillan.

Carr, F., and Cope, S. (1994). Britain and Europe: From Community to Union? In Savage, S.P., Atkinson, R., and Robins, L. (Eds.). *Public Policy in Britain*. London: Macmillan.

Cesarani, D., and Fulbrook, M. (1996). Introduction. In Cesarani, D., and Fulbrook, M. *Citizenship, Nationality and Migration in Europe*. London: Routledge.

Chrisities, K. (1995). *Problems in European Politics*. Chicago: Nelson Hall.

Corrin, C. (1998). The Politics of Gender. In White, S., Batt, J., and Lewis, P.G. (Eds.). *Developments in Central and East European Politics*. Basingstoke: Macmillan.

Cox, T. (1998). The Politics of Social Change in Transformation. In White, S., Batt, J., and Lewis, P.G. (Eds.). *Developments in Central and East European Politics*. Basingstoke: Macmillan.

Dickens, P., and Oberg, S. (1996). The Global Context: Europe in a World of Dynamic and Population Change. *European Urban and Regional Studies*, 3(2): pp 101–120.

Dobrinsky, R. (1996). Enterprise Restructuring and Adjustment in the Transition to Market

Economy: Lessons from the Experience of Central and Eastern Europe. *Economics of Transition*, Vol. 4(2): pp 389–410.

Feigenbaum, C., and Norpoth, L. (1995). *Politics and Government in Europe Today*. Boston: Houghton Mifflin Company.

Guterres, A. (1998). Closer Financial European Integration and the Consequences of the Single Currency. *Economic and Financial Review*, Winter: pp 153–156.

Gallagher, T. (1998). The Balkans: Bulgaria, Romania, Albania and the Former Yugoslavia. In White, S., Batt, J., and Lewis, P.G. (Eds.). *Developments in Central and East European Politics*. Basingstoke: Macmillan.

Harris, G. (1999). The Extreme Right in Contemporary Europe. *Politics Review*, February: pp 8–10.

Healey, N. (1996). The Economics of Transition: From Marx to the Market. *Economic Review*, September: pp 4–9.

Jackman, R. (1998). The Impact of the European Union on Unemployment and Unemployment Policy. In Hines, D., and Kassim, H. (Eds.). *Beyond the Market: The EU and National Social Policy*. London: Routledge.

Lane, C. (1998). Industrial Structure and Performance: Common Challenges—Diverse Experiences. In Bailey, J. (Ed.). *Social Europe*. London: Longman.

Lawrence, P. (1996). European Security: A New Era of Crisis? In Bideleux, R., and Taylor, R. (Eds.). *European Integration and Disintegration, East and West*. London: Routledge.

Lewis, P.G. (1998). East-Central Europe: The Czech Republic, Slovakia, Hungary and Poland. In White, S., Batt, J., and Lewis, P.G. (Eds.). *Developments in Central and East European Politics*. Basingstoke: Macmillan.

Miall, H. (1994). Wider Europe, Fortress Europe, Fragmented Europe? In Miall, H. (Ed.). *Redefining Europe: New Patterns of Conflict and Cooperation*. London: Royal Institute of Internal Affairs.

Millard, F. (1996). Poland's 'Return to Europe', 1989–94. In Bideleux, R., and Taylor, R. (Eds.). *European Integration and Disintegration, East and West*. London: Routledge.

Munday, B. (1998). The Old and the New: Changes in Social Care in Central and Eastern Europe. In Munday, B., and Lane, G. (Eds.). *The Old and the New: Changes in Social Care in Central and Eastern Europe*. Kent: European Institute of Social Services.

Rhodes, M. (1998). Defending the Social Contract: The EU Between Global Constraints and Domestic Imperitives. In Hine, D., and Kassim, H. (Eds.). *Beyond the Market: The EU and National Social Policy*. London: Routledge.

Rose, R. (1997). What is Europe? The Changing Idea of a Continent. *Politics Review*, January: pp 26–30.

Smith, G. (1992). Soviet Endgames: Nationalities and the End of the Soviet Union. *Politics Review*, pp 19–22.

Taras, R. (1998). The Politics of Leadership in Poland. In White, S., Batt, J., and Lewis, P.G. (Eds.). *Developments in Central and East European Politics*. Basingstoke: Macmillan.

White, S., Batt, J., and Lewis, P.G. (Eds.). *Developments in Central and East European Politics*. Basingstoke: Macmillan.

William, T. (1995) cited in Lawrence (1996). European Security: A New Era of Crisis? In Bideleux, R., and Taylor, R. (Eds.). *European Integration and Disintegration, East and West*. London: Longman.

Chapter 3

Child Prostitution
in England

Tim Lenihan and Penny Dean

Introduction

Child prostitution is not a new phenomenon in Britain, although it should be noted that the examples used throughout this chapter are primarily drawn from England, (see Chapter 9 for the different legal system for young people in Scotland). In the early part of the 19th century voluntary organisations were working with children selling sex, (Hawkes, 1982), and child prostitution became a matter of great concern to the late Victorians, whose reforming zeal and pioneering child welfare legislation set the boundaries of what we now call childhood.

Creating childhood, as the Victorians effectively did, meant protecting children, and the same period saw a reform of child employment law and the introduction of compulsory education. This was the period that saw the start of the public health movement which took an interest in, among other things, promoting the health of children by passing the vaccinations acts of 1840, 1853 and 1867, (Porter, 1999). It was also the great age of the philanthropic movements, which gave birth to the children's charities, many of which are still running today.

After the turn of the century, public concern about children involved in prostitution in Britain appears to have vanished and only began to resurface in the 1980s. Charities working with young runaways noticed that a significant minority of children who had run away from home or care, were selling sex to survive. Research carried out and published by The Children's Society about young runaways, and confirmed by Home Office figures, showed that around 4,000 children and young people were cautioned and convicted for offences relating to prostitution between 1989 and 1995, (Lee and O'Brien, 1995).

Prostitution in Britain is not an offence, although the law penalises related activities such as loitering, soliciting and living off immoral earnings. Under the 1959 Street Offences Act, the law makes no distinction between adults and children selling sex and sees them both as equally culpable. Clearly, laws which assume that children and young people can actively and of their own free will, engage in prostitution, are inconsistent with laws on the age of consent, presently 16 for heterosexual and 18 for homosexual sex in Britain, and child protection legislation.

This failure of the 1959 Act to distinguish between adults and children is, arguably, a reflection of the willingness of a public (and a parliament) to ignore the reality of child prostitution. The result is a legislative confusion, which allows children to be prosecuted for offences related to prostitution, before they are legally able to consent to sexual intercourse. To put it another way, the 1959 Act legislates for children to be punished for being abused. It was the application of this anomalous law that The Children's Society highlighted when it published the number of cautions and convictions of children in *The Game's Up*, (1995).

One result of treating children in prostitution as offenders has been to absolve the adults who abuse them. Police, whose job after all is to uphold the law, are unable to free the time and resources to protect children the law brands as criminals, while others are unwilling to accept that children are not acting by their own free will. Even where the police wish to prosecute adult offenders, collecting evidence against them is expensive and time consuming. Children and young people are often reluctant to give evidence against adults on whom they may depend for financial survival, while fear of violent reprisal and an understandable distrust of the authorities make them unwilling witnesses.

Defining 'prostitution' also adds complexity to an already difficult picture. As evidence about children in prostitution has mounted, it has become clear that child prostitution can operate on an informal basis. A definition of child prostitution needs to encompass the young runaway who exchanges sex for a bed and a roof over one's head for the night, as well as a child exchanging sex for some form of payment such as money, drink, drugs and other consumer goods.

History of Child Prostitution and Scope

Child prostitution was in evidence enough for the Society for the Prevention of Juvenile Prostitution to be active throughout the early 1800s. Concern about child prostitution gained momentum in late Victorian Britain, when, after a public outcry about the plight of children in prostitution, legislation was passed to protect children and prevent their involvement. As a result of this lobbying, a new law was passed in 1874 setting the minimum legal age of prostitution at 12. The age was raised to 13 years in 1875 and finally to 16 in 1885, (Lee and O'Brien, 1995).

The Industrial Schools Amendment Bill in 1880, gave courts the power to remove children from home or the streets and place them in industrial schools if they were considered to be living depraved lives or associating with prostitutes. In 1881, Edward Rudolf, a Sunday School teacher and civil servant, founded the Waifs and Strays, now known as The Children's Society. In its first decade, 356 girls were referred to the Society's industrial schools, of whom 40 per cent were either residing with a prostitute or frequenting the company of prostitutes, (ibid).

In 1885, The Pall Mall Gazette, a popular London newspaper of the time, exposed child prostitution and the white slave trade, sparking off a public movement to protect children. An editorial in The Times in June that year welcomed the new proposal to raise the age of consent, but warned that a simple legal response to the problem of child prostitution would ignore the underlying causes that led to children's involvement in prostitution.

In recent years the debates have resurfaced. In 1981, on the centenary of its foundation, The Children's Society carried out research to find the needs of young homeless people. The result was the Central London Teenage Project (CLTP), which opened in 1985 as a refuge for young runaways. In its first two years, the project saw 532 children, of whom seven per cent had been involved in prostitution since they had been on the street. Other streetwork projects and refuges opened in Bournemouth, Manchester, Leeds and Birmingham, their findings corroborating the experience of CLTP.

Building on its findings, The Children's Society's task was to convince a sceptical public that had forgotten the lessons the Victorians had learnt; namely that children in Britain were involved in prostitution. Around this time, there was increasing public concern about child sex tourism abroad, particularly in the Far East where the streets of Bangkok reputedly gave paedophiles a free rein to abuse children. Comments about the problem in Britain, however, were largely restricted to a few pronouncements of disbelief.

In 1992, The National Children's Homes, now NCH Action for Children, published their research, *Runaways: Exploding the Myths*, that estimated that 43,000 children run away each year, (Stein, Abrahams and Mungall, 1992). This was followed in 1994 when The Children's Society published a report into child runaways called *Running—The Risk*, (Stein, Rees and Frost, 1994), in which children who came to projects in Bournemouth, Newport, Leeds, Manchester and Birmingham were questioned about their survival strategies on the street. Of 102 children questioned, 15 said they had sold sex in order to survive. The report estimated that 10,000 children ran away more than ten times by the time they were sixteen.

In 1995 The Children's Society launched a campaign, *The Game's Up*, aimed to persuade the British public to examine problems closer to home. The campaign's goals included changing the attitudes of professionals so that children involved in prostitution are treated as victims of abuse instead of criminals. *The Game's Up* published, for the first time, the Home Office police figures for cautions and convictions of children involved in prostitution and called for new legislation to protect children from being charged. Using the only statistical records available—the number of children cautioned or convicted for offences relating to child prostitution—the significant traffic in children selling sex became apparent. Between 1989 and 1995, there were 2,380 cautions issued and 1,730 convictions secured in England and Wales against young people under the age of 18. The figures included the caution of one ten year old child.

Continuing its campaign, in 1997 The Children's Society published *Child Prostitution: Dilemmas and Practical Responses*, (Barrett, 1997), which examined the experience of professionals working in the field, and launched the first national conference on child prostitution. It was accompanied by a provocative advertising campaign designed to jolt the public out of its denial of the reality of child prostitution. Picturing a beach on a tourist destination in the Far East it asked: *Why travel six thousand miles to have sex with children when you can do it in Britain?* The campaign did the trick attracting hostility and support in equal measure and sparked off a national debate.

Other charities also campaigned to highlight the level of child prostitution in Britain. In Autumn 1996, Barnardo's launched its Streets and Lanes project which worked with children forced into prostitution. Barnardo's had already began outreach work in King's Cross with its SOLD-IT project in the mid 1990s. In 1999, it published a report *Whose Daughter Next?*, (Barnardo's, 1998), which reported on 100 girls and young women aged between 12 and 17 who had been coerced into prostitution. Almost half of them were under the age of consent; more than one third lived at home with their parents; 14 per cent were in care or accommodated. The report found that a total of forty-eight agencies had contact, with a minimum of 267 girls under 16 and 338 females aged 16–18 who were involved in prostitution.

Some social services departments also began to investigate the level of children involved in prostitution in their locality. In Wiltshire, a rural county in the South West of England, the social services department's emergency duty team logged 37 calls from children involved in prostitution over a seven month period, including calls from 12 year olds, (Wiltshire County Council, 1998). The report did not include calls from Swindon, by far the largest town in the county. Between 1989 and 1993, Home Office records show that there were only three cautions and twenty five convictions of children involved in prostitution in Wiltshire. None of these were issued to children under the age of 16. These figures add to the weight of evidence collected by experts from all agencies which suggests that the number of cautions and convictions represent only a small proportion of the actual figure of children involved in prostitution.

In 1995, as a result of *The Game's Up* campaign, the Association of Police Officers (ACPO) and the Association of Directors of Social Services issued statements calling for children involved in prostitution to be treated as victims of abuse, rather than be criminalised. Following this statement, ACPO then put into place pilot schemes to test the policy. Two child sexual exploitation pilot projects were set up by ACPO, one in Nottingham and another in Wolverhampton, to treat child prostitution as a child protection matter. An interim report on the projects revealed its successes: 'A substantial amount of child sexual exploitation has been uncovered. This was previously unreported or not recognised. Simply changing staff awareness, staff attitudes and working practices in all of the concerned agencies has had a dramatic effect on policing child sexual exploitation', (Brain *et al.*, 1998).

The report added that many of the children had 'extremely complex' problems and argued that further consideration needed to be given to the development of exit strategies and support systems for children who were at risk of sexual exploitation. The pilot project in Wolverhampton reported working with 40 children aged between 11 and 17 over a six month period between August, 1997 and February, 1998. This compared with 43 cautions and 32 convictions in the whole of the West Midlands Police Authority in 1993 for a whole year. As a result of dealing with children under child protection procedures, they had amassed evidence resulting in nine adults being charged with serious criminal offences including rape, unlawful sexual intercourse, attempting to procure a child for unlawful sexual intercourse, kidnap, unlawful imprisonment, witness intimidation and assault. Further prosecutions are pending.

In Nottinghamshire, in the 12 months following January, 1997, police reported 40 females and 12 males who had come into contact with police officers at the pilot scheme and were between 10 and 17 years old. The reasons for being involved in prostitution were listed as; already involved in other crimes, non-attendance at school, previous abuse, coercion into prostitution by boyfriend, drug addiction, poverty and homelessness.

In December, 1998, the Home Office and the Department of Health issued guidelines for consultation about how police should deal with children caught up in prostitution. The guidance aims to raise an awareness of children caught up in prostitution, to inform agencies about the nature of the problem and to ensure that health, police and local authorities adopt consistent policies to treat children primarily as victims of abuse. The guidelines acknowledge that 'There are children involved in prostitution in many parts of Britain. They may not be visible to a casual or even an informed observer. They may not be obvious on the streets. But there will be children being abused through prostitution in rooms and flats in many towns. This is a hidden problem; we do not know how many children are involved. We can, however, be certain that this problem exists', (Home Office, 1998). The guidance also aimed to promote multi-agency work to provide children with strategies to exit prostitution as well as to investigate and prosecute those who coerce, exploit and abuse children.

Although warmly welcomed by most agencies working with children involved in prostitution, the guidelines still allow the police to retain the powers of cautioning and prosecuting 'voluntary and persistent' children who, it is argued, freely choose to 'solicit, loiter or opportune in a public place for the purposes of prostitution', (Home Office, 1998: Section 5.15). In such cases the police are entitled to start criminal justice proceedings where diversion has failed.

This paragraph raises concerns about what 'voluntary and persistent' means in context of children in prostitution. Although the guidelines are clear that the presumption should not be made that the child is soliciting freely, there is a concern from children's charities that this recommendation does not fully acknowledge the difficulties children have in exiting prostitution. Research overwhelmingly suggests that children involved in selling sex have had damaged and chaotic lives. Sexual and physical abuse, poverty, rejection, drug dependence and coercion into prostitution by manipulative and dangerous adults are some of the experiences that children often cite. The more difficult the young person's problems, the more difficult it is for a young person to exit prostitution. The objection to the recommendation about voluntary and persistent offending is not merely that it fails to recognise the problem of exiting prostitution, but that it is in principle unacceptable to suggest that a child or young person should be cautioned or convicted for being abused.

The Children's Society, Barnardo's and the NSPCC remain convinced that the only logical and moral decision in such circumstances is an overhaul of sexual offences legislation which recognises once and for all in law that children involved in prostitution are victims of abuse and the offences relating to children under 18 in prostitution should be removed from statute.

Models of Entry into Child Prostitution

The guidelines raise an important issue that has been at the centre of a debate; how do young people become involved in prostitution? The two main models both make it clear that however children become involved, they have little choice in the matter. Research by The Children's Society suggests that poverty is the main cause of prostitution. According to this model, prostitution is a survival strategy for children and young people. Some have run away from home and turned to theft, drugs or selling sex to survive. Many come from chaotic and disturbed backgrounds. A significantly high proportion have suffered physical or sexual abuse. Increasingly, young people are involved in drug abuse at a worryingly early age, either before they become involved in prostitution, or after, as a way of seeking solace. In *Running—The Risk*, as many as a quarter had been physically and/or sexually assaulted whilst on the streets. Many others had indulged in self-harm and suicide attempts. Poverty was identified as the main cause given by interviewees for becoming involved in prostitution in a 1999 study commissioned by The Children's Society. In this study, *One Way Street*, (Melrose, Barrett and Brodie, 1999), approximately three-quarters of the interviewees said their main reason for getting involved was lack of money. Half of them said they went into prostitution as a survival strategy, while half said they wanted things they would not have been able to afford without working. Undoubtedly the financial rewards are an incentive for young people who have lived in deprivation, while some express a sense of power when their self esteem is boosted by meeting a punter who is prepared to pay for them.

As well as those citing money as their main reason for becoming involved in prostitution, over a quarter said their main reason was to get drugs. Most of those who gave this answer were under 25 years old. High levels of drug use has been previously well documented amongst young people involved in prostitution and it would be extremely worrying if this recent research which shows that young people are more likely to get involved because of drugs, is part of a larger trend. One interesting fact to emerge from this study was that almost twice as many children started using drugs *after* getting involved in prostitution than got into prostitution as a result of a drug habit.

Causes for entry into prostitution are notoriously complex, and even where a drug habit can be cited as a reason for entry into prostitution, or a reason for continuing in prostitution, a broader, damaged picture often emerges:

Nicki, who was 14 at the time of the interview, had become involved in prostitution the previous year. She had first been looked after when she was five after her mother had left her and her younger siblings with their violent alcoholic and drug addicted father. Nicki was then adopted when she was ten and in the process had been separated from two of her siblings. A year after she was adopted, Nicki's natural father died from a drugs overdose after which she started 'being naughty'. She was returned to care by her adoptive parents and became involved in prostitution when she ran away with a friend. She said: 'I thought it were good at first but then I didn't want to go down there again [to the beat]. But I had to for drugs.

(Ibid: p 26)

Although most of those who became involved in prostitution for financial reasons had chaotic backgrounds, some also felt empowered by prostitution. Punters made them feel special. They saw their income as a measure of their value, while their spending power compared to their peers was seen as a measure of their success. Others talked of the 'buzz' of not being caught and felt powerful in relation to the 'punters'. This 'buzz' needs to be measured against abusive or neglectful family backgrounds which often results in low self esteem and a desire for empowerment of any sort which attaches some sort of value to their life. Being 'desired' can be seen as a substitute for being loved.

This response needs to be measured against the added risks to sexual health, drug use and violence from punters and perhaps it is because the monetary transaction is the one area of life that they feel they have control over that they invest so much importance in it:

You knew they were coming for you. You could tell them when to stop and when to go. And they were giving you things. They had to buy you. They couldn't just have you. They bought you because you were special. It made you feel a bit like mmm, you know? And that's a big feeling.

(Melrose, Barrett and Brodie, 1999: p 29)

Damaged self esteem can be measured in the prevalence of sexual and physical abuse amongst children involved in prostitution. The same report questioned 50 adults who had sold sex as children. Nearly three quarters of them had experienced conflict or abuse in their families. Of these, half had been sexually abused in the home. For almost half of those questioned, sexual abuse was their first sexual experience. Thirteen reported having their first sexual experience before they were ten.

A second model, which has been prevalent in a project run by Barnardo's, is that young people are 'groomed' by older youths. These young men aged typically between 18 and 25 target vulnerable younger girls usually between 12 and 14 and shower them with gifts and affection, gradually gaining an emotional hold over them. They then begin a sexual relationship. His age and wealth confer status on the girl who is then dependent on the older man. Once the pimp has achieved a hold on the girl, he takes control of her life, forces her to work for him and threatens her with physical violence. Finally the 'boyfriend' gains total dominance over the girl's life. He asks her to do 'sexual favours' for his friends to prove her love to him and begins earning money from her services. The girl, now ensnared, may be 'sold on' to another man while her old boyfriend moves in on another vulnerable girl. This model is based on work carried out by Barnardo's Streets and Lanes Project in Bradford and has a historical precedent. In 1836 the French traveller and observer Flora Tristan wrote in the 1836 annual report of the Society for the Prevention of Juvenile Prostitution:

> *As soon as the female has been decoyed to a brothel, she is no longer allowed to wear her own clothes, which become the prize of the keeper; she is decked with second hand trappings, once the property of some wealthy lady. The regular clients are notified, but when she no longer attracts customers to the house, her master sends her to walk the streets, where he has her closely watched so that it is impossible for her to escape, and if she attempts it, the spy, usually a bully or a procuress, charges her with stealing from the master of the house, the clothes she wears on her back.*

(In Hawkes, 1982)

Recent research commissioned by The Children's Society suggests that although there clearly is evidence that some young girls are 'groomed' into prostitution by pimps or 'boyfriends', most young people are introduced into prostitution by their peers, usually as part of a last chapter in a complex story in which a damaged young person has suffered a range of indignities including poverty and/or abuse.

The increase in poverty in Britain throughout the 1970s and 1980s is well documented. During these decades the gap between rich and poor widened; housing and social security policies penalised those living in poverty, while high levels of unemployment added financial strain on those families. During the 1980s, the average income of council households fell from 75 per cent of the national average to 49 per cent. A 1995 study found that 50 per cent of council dwellings had no wage earner. The number of heroin users throughout the 1980s increased, with 12,000 users officially registered and an estimated number of 50–60,000 using the drug. A study by Centrepoint revealed that within six weeks, most young people living on the streets would resort to crime, drugs and/or prostitution as a survival mechanism, (Joseph Rowntree Foundation, 1996).

In April, 1988, the government withdrew the right of 16 and 17 year olds to claim state benefit, which confronted young people who had run away with the choice of returning from the home they had run from, and where many had suffered physical, sexual or emotional abuse, or surviving by their wits on the streets. In the 18 months following the implementation of the 1988 act, the number of 16–19 year olds without proper accommodation in London had increased by 35 per cent, (Barrett, 1997: p 147). Restoring benefits to 16 and 17 year olds remains a priority for The Children's Society and other charities who see benefits as a way of preventing children being forced into prostitution.

There are currently around 150,000 16 to 17 year olds who are out of training, work or education, and it is these un-engaged young people who are most at risk of drifting out of mainstream society and to disappear into a world of crime, drugs or prostitution. The new Labour Government has pledged to attack social inequalities and the 1999 March budget was estimated by the Chancellor of the Exchequer, Gordon Brown, to lift 700,000 children out of poverty. The Social Exclusion Unit has been set up to find ways of re-engaging these young people. In May, 1999, the Chancellor announced a pilot scheme to pay £40 a week to children whose families are living in poverty, to stay on at school. However welcome these developments appear, it is as yet too early to say what their long-term benefits for children will be.

In order to be successful, the government will need to buck a trend of social inequality which is increasing and, according to a 1996 report by the United Nations Development Programme, is 'now as extreme as it is in Nigeria', (Townsend, 1996). An estimated 33 per cent of children now live in poverty, (ibid).

Residential Care and Child Prostitution

Research has consistently examined the relationship between children in prostitution and children in care. In 1991, Birmingham Social Services commissioned a report into young people in care involved in prostitution. The report, *The Social Services Care System and Juvenile Prostitution: Young Women in Care*, (Jesson, 1991), was prompted in 1985 after a working party set up by Birmingham Social Services concluded that there were 15 young people on the register who 'are thought to be or have been involved in sexual activity for financial benefit'. They suggested that another 22 young women were suspected, or at risk of involvement. The subsequent report estimated that between October, 1990 and July, 1991, 20 young women in care between the ages of 13 and 18 were believed to be involved in prostitution. Most were between 14 and 16 years old. Half the young women were known to have a history of sexual abuse and three others were suspected of having been sexually abused. Half the women had absconded from home before coming into care, a behaviour that was linked to the abuse at home. Some of the girls said they had been raped. Six had contracted sexually transmitted diseases and four had become pregnant. The report was printed, but all copies were destroyed by the Social Services Department for fear of the controversy the report would cause.

The Children's Society's recent study, *One Way Street*, revealed that half those interviewed about their experience as a young person in prostitution had been in care and half of those had a history of going missing from care. Moreover, the study suggested that the proportion of young people involved in prostitution who have been in care is increasing.

This does not mean that residential care is necessarily to blame for the drift into prostitution, after all, children in care are more likely to have had disrupted and damaged lives than others. One study, (Stein, *Going Missing*, 1986), found that of 36 young people in care, ten were involved in prostitution. Eight had been sexually abused before going into care, while nine had suffered physical abuse, neglect or rejection by their families. Nine of them exhibited behavioural difficulties such as self-destructiveness, low sense of self worth and aggressive tendencies. All of them, bar one, had been drawn into prostitution while being looked after. Peer pressure, particularly in residential settings, is often cited as an entry into prostitution and as one young woman in care said, 'If you're in care with a prostitute they'll try to get you to go out with them. If not, then you get bullied from them', (Stein, 1986). Sometimes this pressure is accompanied by threats.

Residential care staff can find themselves powerless to act against exploitative adults, or pimps hanging out outside the home to recruit children and many staff feel they lack the skills or knowledge required to intervene on behalf of the child. Where social workers were unable to contain the problem or protect children, they focused on harm reduction, such as advising on safe sex. Staff often felt compromised by offering such support while a young person was selling sex, but felt they had no other powers to intervene.

In 1998, Harrow Council was pilloried after the death of Ayilah Ismail following an overdose of methadone. She was 13 years old and had contracted six sexually transmitted diseases. An independent report commissioned by social services revealed that she had been passed on to over 200 staff during her time in care.

The Legal Picture

The law in Britain about sexual offences is confused and is currently undergoing a government review. Currently, the legal age of consent is 16 for heterosexual sex and 18 for homosexual sex, although parliament is expected to vote to lower the age of consent for homosexuals in the near future. The debate about the age of consent has been deliberately excluded from the government review. According to Cityboys, a charity based in Manchester working with young gay men who have run away from home, one possible impact of this law could be to prevent the stigmatisation and prejudice against young gay men, which plays a factor in their running away, and lessen the risk of drifting into prostitution in order to survive.

The legal framework for current policing on prostitution was set in the 1959 Street Offences Act that gave police and the court powers to convict a common prostitute for loitering and soliciting. Guidelines issued at the time advised police to issue two warnings, or cautions, before making an arrest. Under this legislation, men could also be charged as a 'common prostitute', but in May, 1994 the high court ruled that only women could be charged with loitering for the purposes of prostitution under the 1959 Act.

Prostitution is not illegal, but soliciting, loitering, living off immoral earnings, running a brothel and procuring are. The Act does not make a distinction in law between adults and children and young people.

Section 12 of the 1956 Sexual Offences Act makes it an offence to commit buggery with another person unless both parties are over the age of 18 *and* the act takes place in private. The law makes no distinction between consensual acts and non-consensual acts or whether or not the sex was paid for.

Penalties for sexual offences unintentionally offer greater protection to boys than girls who are over 13 and under 16. Under Section 5 of the 1956 Sexual Offences Act, unlawful sexual intercourse with a girl under 13 carries a maximum sentence of life imprisonment. Yet Home Office records contain figures showing that a 10 year old girl was cautioned for prostitution in 1992. Under section 12 of the same Act, buggery and attempted buggery, with an animal or a person under 16 carries a maximum sentence of life imprisonment.

But under Section 6 of the Act, unlawful sexual intercourse with a girl under 16 only carries a maximum penalty of two years imprisonment. Section 14 of the Act makes it an offence to make an indecent assault on a woman. All sexual activity with girls under 16, whether consensual or not, is considered indecent assault. The maximum penalty is five years imprisonment if a child is under 13 and two years if between 13 and 16. Section 15 makes it an offence to make an indecent assault on a man, which includes young males under 18. All homosexual sex with a male is indecent assault and carries a maximum penalty of 10 years. Under this law, then, young women are not able to give consent, but the punishment for abusing them is relatively minor compared to the punishment against boys. Ironically, a discriminatory piece of legislation against young gay men has resulted in greater protection for young women. The result is that adults who are abusing girls in prostitution have far less to fear from the law than those abusing boys.

Child prostitution in Britain has until recently been a much neglected topic, and while recent research has given a clearer picture about the causes of prostitution and the entry and exit points for children caught up in prostitution, policy and practice is, with the exception of a handful of voluntary organisations, far behind.

Currently there are only two refuges in England providing support for young runaways, who are among the most vulnerable of young people. As we have seen, these are some of the children who are most at risk of being exploited by dangerous adults and of ending up in prostitution. The Children's Society runs one of these refuges which is funded entirely from voluntary donations. The Society is in the process of expanding its refuge and streetwork projects. The NSPCC and Centrepoint run the third refuge, which until recently received financial support from the Department of Health until it was removed before the last election. Streetwork projects providing outreach support also provide points of contact with young people involved in selling sex, while the success of Barnardo's Streets and Lanes project has led to the opening of five similar projects in England.

These initiatives are vital, but are necessarily piecemeal. The government has pledged its support for finding ways of funding refuges, but has yet to come up with any concrete support. The government response to the Children's Safeguards Review in 1998, section 2.21, says:

> *The government also recognises the importance of refuges that cater for young people. It will work constructively with local government and voluntary bodies to strengthen their role and financial basis.*

Refuges are expensive and require 24 hour staffing, but they deal with some of the young people most at risk of violent attack, rape, sexual assault, self harm and even murder.

The new police guidelines issued by the Home Office and the Department of Health will provide more support for young people involved in prostitution and increase prosecution of adult offenders as the pilot studies have shown.

Residential care staff have expressed their powerlessness and lack of training about how to deal with children who persistently return to prostitution despite the best efforts of staff. Police claim their right to caution and prosecute children for offences relating to prostitution, will in some cases, protect children. However, organisations in the field point to the positive results of working with young people, rather than treating them as criminals, which has led to positive outcomes for both the young people and the police targeting the adults who abuse the children.

Benefit changes are crucial in the prevention of children being caught up in prostitution, and the restitution of benefits for 16–17 year olds is one of the most important changes the government could make. This is not just for children in prostitution, but to re-engage all children who are slipping through the welfare net, who are not in work, training or education and who are at risk of turning to crime, including prostitution, without the necessary financial support to survive.

Conclusion

The last ten years have seen a willingness to confront the issue of child prostitution in Britain. However, there is a particular shortage of material about how young males become involved in prostitution. Working patterns for boys and young men appear to be different; there is no pimping system. Unlike consenting individuals in heterosexual relationships, gay men live in a world that is used to using subterfuge in order to avoid homophobia. Young men who sell sex are particularly reluctant to contact agencies. Offenders face higher penalties under the law and perhaps greater caution is exercised to prevent discovery. Male prostitution is also less visible; young men do not walk the streets, nor do they operate in massage parlours. Often they are independent and isolated outside their own community.

Nevertheless, the public awareness campaign has been won, and there can be few people who continue to deny that the problem of child prostitution exists in Britain. This acknowledgement alone supports voluntary organisations to pressurise governments or to fundraise to provide services which would not exist without them.

The public awareness campaign mirrors the reaction to child sexual abuse when it was first raised; shock is followed by denial which gives way to outrage. Gradually there is an acceptance of the problem, a willingness to confront the issues followed by institutional action to develop preventative work and to safeguard the victims.

Now that the problem of child prostitution in Britain has resurfaced, it is essential that all agencies involved take action. Unless services, such as streetwork projects, refuges and specialist services to help children exit prostitution, are set up, there is a danger that the issue will briefly engage the interest of various agencies and then vanish from view, just as it did at the end of the last century. We now need creative strategic thinking about exit routes and to ensure that children and young people have access to support and can avoid the brutal, long term emotional and physical health problems which are so often a consequence of child prostitution. Such services require a multi-disciplinary approach to deal with the complex issues that child prostitution presents.

The myth that child prostitution only goes on abroad has been seriously dented. But developments in the European community will increase trade of all kinds in the coming years, and we need to ensure that multi-agency work has an international dimension to ensure that we do not allow children to become another commodity in the liberalisation of trade in the community. Already, with the collapse of the Eastern Bloc, reports of adults selling sex and migrating over the border to richer neighbours have become apparent. As some of the research referred to in this chapter makes clear, where there are gulfs between the rich and poor, prostitution is likely to flourish and children are likely to be involved.

The international dimension of child prostitution must not allow us to forget the problem that exists within Britain. Children are involved in prostitution in Britain, and the evidence is that the numbers can be measured not in hundreds, but in thousands. That is not to say there is an epidemic or that there has necessarily been a massive increase in child prostitution, but it does mean that thousands of children every year are being lost to the welfare system as they begin a nightmare ride from poverty to abuse. Many of these children are still not getting the help they need, because there are still those who deny the problem exists. As one speaker remarked at a recent conference on children involved in prostitution, 'If there is one local authority in this country which says it does not have a problem of child prostitution, then they aren't looking closely enough'.

References

Barnardo's (1999). *Whose Daughter Next?* Essex: Barnardo's.

Barrett, D. (Ed.) (1997). *Child Prostitution in Britain: Dilemmas and Practical Responses.* The Children's Society.

Brain, T. *et al.* (1998). *Child Prostitution: A Report on the ACPO Guidelines and the Pilot Studies in Wolverhampton and Nottinghamshire.* Gloucester Constabulary.

Hawkes, J. (Ed.) (1982). *The London Journals of Flora Tristan.* Virago.

Home Office. *Draft Guidance on Children Involved in Prostitution.* Home Office, 29th December, 1998, Section 1.2.

Jesson, J. (1991). *The Social Services Care System and Juvenile Prostitution: Young Women in Care*, (unpublished).

Joseph Rowntree Foundation (1996). *The Future of Work: Contributions to the Debate.* Joseph Rowntree Foundation.

Lee, M. and O'Brien, R. (1995). *The Game's Up.* The Children's Society.

Melrose, M., Barrett, D. and Brodie, I. (1999). *One Way Street: Retrospectives on Child Prostitution.* The Children's Society.

Porter, D. (1999). *Health, Civilisation and the State.* Routledge.

Stein, M., Abrahams, C. and Mungall, R. (1992). *Runaways: Exploding the Myths.* National Children's Homes.

Stein, M., Rees, G. and Frost, N. (1994). *Running—The Risk: Young People on the Streets in Britain Today.* The Children's Society.

Townsend, P. (1996). *A Poor Future.* London: Lemos and Lane.

Wade, J., Biehal, N., with Clayden, J., and Stein, M. (1998). *Going Missing: Young People Absent from Care.* Chichester: Wiley.

Wiltshire County Council. Press Release, October 15th, 1998.

Chapter 4

Child Prostitution in Ireland: A Hidden Problem

Simon Brooke

Changes in Irish Society

Ireland has a reputation as a poor, conservative country, with a very strong commitment to the nuclear family. However, recent changes in Irish society have underlined the inaccuracy of this stereotype.

The Irish economy has performed extraordinarily well during the last decade, after a long period of poor performance. Economic growth is substantially higher than any other EU country; interest rates and inflation are extremely low; and unemployment, which has been the major social and economic issue over the last twenty years or so, is now falling steadily.

One of the side effects of this economic success is that house prices have more than doubled in the last five years. This is fine for people who already have a mortgage or own their house outright, but a serious problem for those who do not. Rents in the private rented sector have followed house prices, putting rented accommodation beyond the reach of many people on low incomes. Government promises to build more local authority and housing association housing have yet to be realised; last year fewer of these houses were built than four years ago.

Despite this general increase in prosperity, poverty is an enduring feature of Irish society. Poverty is notoriously difficult to measure, and comparisons are difficult. However, it can be stated with confidence that substantial numbers of Irish people experience poverty, that the level of poverty did not change much between 1987 and 1994 (more recent data is not yet available) and that there is more poverty in Ireland than Denmark, the Netherlands or Belgium, and less poverty than Portugal or Greece. In 1997, the government launched a National Anti-Poverty Strategy covering the period 1997–2007 which aims to reduce considerably the numbers who are 'consistently poor' from 9–15 per cent to less than 5–10 per cent.

So, at the same time as Ireland is accustoming itself to its new-found wealth— sales of new Mercedes cars are at an all time high, and it is estimated that about 500 houses in Dublin are worth more than IR£1m—homeless hostels are full and homeless children still sleep on city streets.

In recent years, Irish society has become steadily more liberal. In 1978 contraception was legalised; a referendum held in 1992 changed the constitution to allow information on abortion to be published (although abortion itself remains illegal in nearly all circumstances); homosexuality was legalised in 1993; and in 1995 Ireland voted in a referendum to change the constitution to allow for divorce.

During the 1990s, the Catholic Church's hegemony has been undermined by a series of scandals and convictions of priests for sexual abuse over long periods. Very recently, evidence of extreme physical and sexual abuse by brothers and nuns at industrial schools (residential care for children paid for by the government and run by religious orders) during the 50s, 60s and 70s has emerged, and will further humble the church. Whilst the Catholic Church protests against what it calls 'a la carte' Catholicism, in which people choose to accept only some of the Church's teaching, growing numbers of people are doing exactly that.

Irish society has for many years been remarkably homogenous, with very low historical levels of immigration and so a very small ethnic minority population. This is not to say that Ireland has been free from racism; discrimination against travellers, who are Ireland's largest ethnic minority, has been well documented. In recent years however, this homogeneity has been challenged by the arrival of significant numbers of asylum seekers. Ireland is changing, slowly and in part reluctantly, to a more pluralist, more multicultural society.

One indication of just how far Irish society has changed in a short period is that the present Taoiseach (Prime Minister), who is separated from his wife, lives openly in an unmarried relationship with his present partner. This has received remarkably little attention, even though it would have been unthinkable only a few years ago.

Children at Risk

This section briefly outlines some of the current issues relating to children at risk under the following headings: the role of government; poverty; homelessness; children in care; juvenile justice; child abuse and educational disadvantage.

The role of government

Until relatively recently, the government's role in relation to children had been based on outdated legislation, and characterised by a *laissez-faire* approach in which religious bodies played the major role in many aspects of child care.

The Kennedy report on residential childcare in Ireland, which was published in 1970, represented a turning point, recommending major changes in the provision of residential childcare and new legislation. The proposal for new legislation had a gestation of elephantine proportions and the Child Care Act 1991 (the first piece of child welfare legislation enacted since the foundation of the state) did not appear on the statute books for 21 years, and was not fully enacted until 1996. This legislation gives each health board (a regional state body providing health and social services) a legal duty to promote the welfare of children who are not receiving care and protection. Health boards are required to regard the welfare of the child as the first and paramount consideration, having regard to the rights and duties of parents. It has been widely welcomed as progressive legislation with the potential to make a major contribution to improved childcare services, subject to adequate resources being made available.

In 1992, Ireland ratified the UN Convention on the Rights of the Child. Several bodies have recommended that children's express rights be written into the Irish constitution, including the Constitutional Review Group in 1996. This however remains an aspiration.

Currently, responsibility for the welfare of children is divided between five departments: Health and Children; Justice Equality and Law Reform; Education and Science; Social, Community and Family Affairs; and Enterprise, Trade and Employment. This has inhibited coherent policy development in relation to children, and there have been many calls for a national child care authority. The recent appointment of a Minister for Children, covering three of these departments, with specific responsibility for development of childcare policy, has assisted in the development of a more co-ordinated policy.

Poverty

Child poverty is an enduring feature of Irish society, which appears to have been left relatively unchanged by the general increasing prosperity in the country at large. One third of all children in Ireland are dependent on welfare support systems and Ireland has the second highest level of child poverty in the EU. In 1998, the UN Committee dealing with the Convention on the Rights of the Child criticised the Irish government for the level of child poverty and urged the government to, 'take immediate steps to tackle the problem of child poverty and make all possible efforts to ensure that all families have adequate resources and facilities'. Further evidence of child poverty comes from the 1994 *Living in Ireland* survey that found children to be at a higher risk of poverty than adults at each of the relevant poverty lines.

Homelessness

Little is known about the extent of child homelessness in Ireland. In 1997 an emergency social work and accommodation service for children in Dublin and surrounding areas received nearly 3,500 referrals. Many children are forced to use this service numerous times, so this probably represents somewhere in the region of 500 different children homeless in this area in 1997.

The Child Care Act 1991 gives health boards a legal duty to provide accommodation for homeless children. However, despite this, arrangements for the referral of homeless children into emergency accommodation are very far from being child-centred, and substantial numbers of children sleep rough because there is nowhere for them to go.

Studies have shown a high level of drugs misuse amongst homeless children and a disturbingly high proportion of homeless children had previously been in the care of the health board.

Children in care

There are about 3,500 children in care in Ireland. About 80 per cent are in foster care or with relatives and the rest in residential care. There has been a major shift away from residential care in favour of foster care in recent years. This policy has received broad support, but health boards are finding it difficult to recruit and support foster parents.

Juvenile justice

About half of all crime in Ireland is committed by people aged under 21. The principle of diverting young people away from the criminal justice system at an early stage, was established in the 1960s with the creation of the Juvenile Liaison Scheme. However, this sits side by side with a largely outdated body of law based on traditional penal punishment.

The current arrangements for custodial provision include places of detention run by the Department of Justice, and 'special schools' that are run by the Department of Education. These may accommodate children who have committed a criminal offence, together with children with behavioural difficulties who are referred simply because there is no other alternative. This is highly undesirable and in effect 'criminalises' children who have never broken the law.

Legislation, which will strengthen the 'diversion' element of juvenile justice is currently being considered by the Oireachtas (Parliament). It has been widely welcomed, and when implemented will, it is hoped, mark a major step forward in the development of a juvenile justice system which focuses on crime prevention and crime reduction rather than punishment.

Child abuse

Reporting of child abuse has risen sharply during this decade, levelling off in the last couple of years. It is not known whether this increase has been due to an increase in the incidence of child abuse, or an increase in its reporting. The largest category of child abuse in the region covering Dublin and neighbouring areas is neglect, followed by sexual abuse, physical abuse and finally emotional abuse.

The current government has agreed in principle to the concept of mandatory reporting of suspected cases of sexual abuse, but it has yet to put this into practice.

Educational disadvantage

School-leaver surveys show that while over 90 per cent of students from upper socio-economic groups reach Leaving Certificate level, only a little over half (53 per cent) of the children from unskilled manual backgrounds reach this stage. Literacy levels, drop-out rates and rates of educational attainment are all disproportionately high among low income working class groups. It is estimated that up to 20,000 young people leave school every year without adequate qualifications. These young people are more likely to be unemployed and suffer poverty.

Child Prostitution in Ireland

The existence of child prostitution in Ireland has been acknowledged only relatively recently. A report, 1997, from the Eastern Health Board, (a regional state body providing health and social services), compared this nascent awareness with the emergence of the issue of child sexual abuse:

> *There are similarities between the way professional awareness [of child prostitution] is now beginning to emerge, and the way child sexual abuse did as a professional issue in the late 1970s and early 1980s.*

However, there was a growing consciousness of the issue during the mid and late 1990s. Projects working with young people at risk became increasingly aware of the existence of child prostitution and suspected that significant numbers of young people were involved. Parallel to this has been a developing recognition of the need to cater for the particular needs of young people involved in prostitution. When a national seminar on child prostitution was held in October, 1998, believed to have been the first on the subject, there was widespread interest shown from across the country.

The recent 'discovery' of the issue has meant that there has been very little research into child prostitution in Ireland. Most material was produced as an offshoot of research into adult prostitution. Research carried out by Toner, (1997), in Dundalk is the only research known in Ireland that looks specifically at issues surrounding children involved in prostitution.

However, despite the relative paucity of material, it is possible, from analysis of existing research and other material, to piece together a general picture of some aspects of child prostitution in Ireland. Although there is little information about its extent, there is widespread agreement about paths into child prostitution and agreement too, about many elements of an appropriate response to the issue.

Extent of Child Prostitution

In most parts of the country there have been no efforts made to discover the extent of child prostitution, and where efforts have been made, many difficulties have been encountered. There are inherent aspects of child prostitution that make it particularly difficult to quantify.

These difficulties start with the definition. O'Sullivan, (1998), observed that if people limited themselves to a narrow definition of prostitution, they might say that prostitution did not exist in their area. However, if the definition was broadened to include under age sexual activity in exchange for drugs or goods, there was general agreement that it was occurring in many areas.

Many commentators have acknowledged that under age sexual activity or sexual abuse are very secret activities and that the younger the person, the more covert the activity. Research has also confirmed 'the hidden nature of the problem', (Toner, 1998). Some researchers also encountered agencies who were safeguarding the confidentiality of their relationship with their clients by, quite understandably, not being forthcoming with information.

Focus Ireland is a large voluntary organisation that runs a range of services for homeless people, including a number of projects targeting children and young adults. These include a drop-in centre, an emergency hostel and an outreach service. Staff are aware that some of the young people they come into contact with are involved in prostitution, perhaps through money or possessions they may have, or areas they may frequent. But they know too, that many young people feel shame and guilt about their involvement in prostitution, and keep it to themselves.

All these factors make it very difficult to arrive at a confident estimate of the extent of child prostitution and suggest that such estimates as exist are very likely to be underestimates. O'Sullivan, (1998), became aware of this as her research was progressing. 'By the end of the study it was clear that there was a lot more activity going on than documented in the report.'

In Autumn, 1996, Barnardo's carried out a small observational study of children on Dublin's streets, (Barnardo's, 1996). They observed children selling sex and a total of 42 young people aged between 12 and 18 were observed soliciting. However, this figure needs to be treated with some caution, since the observations were carried out on a small number of locations and the total observation time was only five hours. Further obscuring the issue, the observations were carried out on three different occasions. However, it is reasonable to suggest that the undercounting consequent on the limited observation would be far greater than the possible double counting; therefore, the overall figure is very likely to be a substantial underestimate.

The Eastern Health Board Working Group's survey referred to earlier, (Eastern Health Board, 1997), identified 57 children involved in prostitution during a two month period. In fact, 10 of these were aged 18, but because they were known to those working in the child care field it was felt appropriate to include them. Of the 57, 32 were girls and 25 boys. The youngest was aged 13. The vast majority were soliciting on the streets, but three girls were believed to be working in massage parlours. Clearly, children working in massage parlours will be less visible and therefore more difficult to identify. The Working Group believed that the figure of 57 was an underestimate. '…if 57 individual children can be identified as being involved in prostitution in a small scale survey, it is reasonable to assume that the extent of the problem is greater.'

O'Sullivan, (1998), estimated that approximately 10–20 young people aged under 20 were involved in prostitution in the Limerick area, and noted that juvenile prostitution was also suspected in a number of other smaller towns in County Clare. Observation by youth workers in Dundalk led to an estimate of at least 12 young people in the area involved in prostitution. Gardai (police) in Waterford estimate that approximately 12 male minors and 15–25 female minors involve themselves in prostitution.

On the basis of the very limited information available, it is not possible to estimate the total number of children in Ireland who are involved in prostitution with any confidence, nor is it possible to know whether or not the problem is a growing one. However, there is widespread and growing acceptance of its existence and the need to make a specific response.

Ways in to Child Prostitution

There have been considerable efforts made to identify factors that increase the likelihood of involvement in prostitution. It is recognised by all, that involvement in prostitution is a complex issue; far too complex to describe by a simple causal relationship. However, a number of studies have identified factors which increase the likelihood of involvement with prostitution and there is widespread agreement about the nature of these factors.

The Eastern Health Board's Working Group, (Eastern Health Board, 1997), identified the following 'pathways into prostitution':

- Being the victim of severe emotional damage, including sexual abuse.
- Having parents with histories of involvement in prostitution.
- Growing up in a criminal sub-culture.
- Sexual confusion/orientation problems.
- Being 'groomed' by paedophiles.

The report went on:

> *Children who belong to dysfunctional families are more likely to become involved in prostitution. These children have low self-esteem with a poor ability to form attachments. Such children are likely to have spent some time in care.*

O'Sullivan, (1998), identified a similar range of factors that influenced involvement in child prostitution:

- Poorly functioning families of origin.
- Parents and siblings involved in prostitution.
- Running away from home, homelessness and placements in care.
- Poverty, social exclusion and long-term unemployment.
- Physical and sexual abuse in childhood or teenage years.
- Alcohol and drug abuse and addictions.
- Poor and undeveloped sense of personal power and boundaries.

She also pointed to the specific roles played by family members:

> *In some cases, young people are introduced to the 'trade' or rather 'exploitation', by parents and other members of their family. In the course of this research, fathers have been reported to act as pimps for their daughters and women involved in prostitution have been identified as training their son or daughter into the 'profession'.* (O'Sullivan, 1998)

Toner, (1998), in her Dundalk study, came to very similar conclusions:

- unstable family background
- history of sexual or physical abuse
- early school leaving
- involvement in drugs, alcohol or petty crime
- second or third generation unemployment
- parental use of alcohol or drugs resulting in violence in the home

McElwee and Lalor, (1997), make matching observations. 'All the individuals interviewed in this study have claimed that their peer group introduced them to prostitution (as distinct from a pimp or a threatening adult).' The following elements constituted a profile of a juvenile prostitute:

- drifting from home and community
- disconnected from school
- lack of self-esteem, helplessness and worthlessness
- sexual abuse and physical abuse

The study also showed a very strong relationship between child prostitution and homelessness. 46 out of the 57 children had or were presently experiencing homelessness.

Quinlan, (1997), also identified a connection between prostitution and homelessness. In his study (mainly adult men, most of whom had previously been child prostitutes), he found that 16 out of 27 male prostitutes had been homeless at some time in their lives. Quinlan states that many young men going into prostitution are exploring their sexuality, and that other young men have issues around violence in the home, institutional care, abuse and homelessness. O'Sullivan, (1998), too, identifies exploration of sexuality as a way into prostitution, noting that in the absence of any safe social meeting places for the gay community, many male juveniles resort to situations which provide them with opportunities to meet gay men, but which simultaneously lead them into encounters with prostitution. Toner, (1998), echoes this: 'Some are young men confused about their sexuality, who have never had a chance to speak to a gay man'.

However, other commentators have said the notion of exploring one's sexuality suggests that there is a certain amount of free will involved, and that this flies in the face of a definition which is based around exploitation.

Nature of Child Prostitution

Money or other reward...

As has already been noted by O'Sullivan, (1998), child prostitution frequently does not involve money changing hands. Toner, (1998), noted this too:

> *There may not be an explicit payment for sex, but there will be rewards such as treats, clothes or a bed for the night if they are out of home.*

McElwee and Lalor, (1997), made a similar observation:

> *...amongst the juvenile population the commodity that changes hands least for acts of prostitution is in fact money. The youths in Waterford City tend to be involved in episodal acts of prostitution for hash, ecstasy or CDs.*

Focus Ireland's outreach staff report that involvement in prostitution may begin in a very informal way, perhaps by going back to a person's home for sex and a bed for the night. Later this may lead to money changing hands. For some people, prostitution may be their only source of income, for others it may be a way of financing a drug habit.

There was mixed evidence of pimping. The extensive use of telephones in Dundalk was suggested as a pointer to organised pimping, however in Waterford, McElwee and Lalor, (1997), observed that there was little evidence for this. The Eastern Health Board study, (1997), was not able to establish the extent to which children soliciting on the streets were being pimped by adults, but there was some evidence to suggest that older women, who were already involved in prostitution, befriended girls and introduced them to prostitution. The study acknowledged that these children were being doubly abused, both by the sexual offender who engages the child and by the abusing adult who acts as the so-called 'pimp'.

Focus Ireland staff report that although organised pimping has been spoken about, they have no firm evidence of this. However, organised pimping is more likely to involve people in prostitution working from a base and so be less visible on the streets and out of the eyes of outreach workers.

Health risks

Many commentators noted the health risks associated with street prostitution. O'Sullivan, (1998), states:

> *A key problem faced by both adults and juveniles was personal safety. People on the streets are at risk of being mugged, at risk from the weather, at risk of becoming involved with people who desire to abuse them. The range of health risks includes HIV and AIDS, and other STDs. There is also the area of psychological and emotional stress which seemed to be a serious issue for people leading a double life and particularly where a dependency on alcohol and drugs resulted in order to alleviate such stress. On the one hand, the dependency on alcohol and drugs was also a contributing risk factor which lead some people into prostitution. And people who went into prostitution often ended up having alcohol or drugs problems as well.*
>
> (O'Sullivan, 1998)

The punter

Unsurprisingly, there is even less information about punters than about the children involved in prostitution. Quinlan, (1997), notes:

> *The punter or stalker, who is usually an adult male, may have many unresolved issues relating to their own sexuality. Most of the male prostitutes in the Gay Men's Health Project report stated that their customers were much older, married, middle class, heterosexual, bisexual or gay. They were politicians, doctors, and professional people.*

There are manifold reasons why they use male prostitutes; for example it may be easier than going to a gay bar or entering into a gay relationship, especially if married with children. A lot of older married men had repressed their gay sexuality especially in younger life, but later found they had to meet other men. Others are living isolated lonely lives, leading them and the others mentioned above, to become involved in high-risk activities. Gay cruising areas are ways that young male prostitutes meet punters, which can be by chance.

Others adults deliberately stalk boys through observations of hostels or hang outs, then introducing themselves by offering money, cigarettes etc. Some move in, but leave when the older man gets tired of them, the boy having been isolated from friends or meeting other gay peers.

Models of Response

Introduction

Although there has been a growing awareness of the existence of child prostitution in Ireland in the late 1990s, very few projects provide services that are specifically designed to cater for the needs of children involved in prostitution. Important elements of these services have been identified, many of which are applicable to any project targeting young people at risk.

There are particular legal difficulties which make a clear response difficult to achieve. For example, the Criminal Law (Sexual Offences) Act 1993 cites the age of consent to sexual activity to be 17 years. Yet under the Child Care Act 1991, a child is an unmarried person under 18 years old. However, child abuse guidelines require that sexual activity by a person under 18 years should be reported to the Gardai as child abuse. Further pending legislation regarding the age for consent to medical treatment, does not apply to children under 16 years old. In addition, as has already been mentioned, many services used by young people target children and young adults thus introducing additional complexity into the situation, since the law relating to children is very different from the law relating to adults.

A guiding principle of service provision is that it is vital to recognise that child prostitution does not take place in isolation from other social and environmental factors and that service provision must reflect that. This means that a commitment to a co-ordinated multi-agency approach is vital.

Prevention

Prevention must be a cornerstone of any strategy for tackling child prostitution. As the Eastern Health Board, (1997), report states:

> *Of course the best solution is to prevent the drift of children into prostitution in the first place. To this end, sight must not be lost of the need to have sufficient early intervention services aimed at children at risk and the prevention of their detachment from school, community and, ultimately, mainstream society.*

O'Sullivan, (1998), argues for prevention through provision of information. 'Increased awareness in children and young people will also assist in increasing the numbers of victims who will seek help.' She also proposes health promotion in schools around issues of safer sex, particularly regarding the spread of HIV/AIDS, other STDs, and risks of unplanned pregnancies.

> *These should be linked to education programmes covering drugs and alcohol abuse, personal safety, peer pressure and personal empowerment. A young person's awareness of their own self-esteem and the ability to say 'no' can at times be their only defence mechanisms when faced with situations of drug abuse and underage sexual activities.*

Services for children involved in prostitution

There are a number of problems involved in establishing a centre-based (i.e. not outreach) service which is specifically directed at children involved in prostitution. Many young people would not perceive themselves as being involved in prostitution; they may well be extremely hesitant about making contact with a dedicated service because this step requires them to explicitly identify themselves as being involved in prostitution. Furthermore, they may be uncertain of what to expect and also may not wish to be seen by others as using such a service.

Many of the elements of an appropriate service for children involved in prostitution are common to general services targeting young people at risk. In addition, early detection of children's involvement in prostitution is essential if they are to avoid becoming trapped. The rapidity with which young people become involved has been observed in other areas. Focus Ireland, which runs an outreach service targeting homeless children and young adults, has seen newly homeless young people becoming involved in petty crime and drugs as well as prostitution within a very short period of becoming homeless. This early detection is likely to take place either through outreach work or generic centre-based work with young people at risk. For all these reasons, a centre-based service for young people involved in prostitution can most appropriately be provided as part of a wider service targeting young people at risk.

O'Sullivan, (1998), underlines this point:

> *In order to avoid risks of identification or stigma by individuals, services should be available within a setting which provides services to all young people and where the juvenile involved or at risk of prostitution would not be easily detected by the general public.*

These arguments do not of course apply to outreach services, where the nature of the contact does not require that the young people identify themselves as being involved in prostitution, and although the contact takes place in public, it is 'invisible'. A two-pronged approach is needed, comprising centre-based services and outreach services. These two are inter-linked and equally important elements of the overall service provision.

In general, the importance of consulting young people about the development of services targeting them, is emphasised by a number of commentators. O'Sullivan suggests that peer involvement in services will create a more accessible and approachable service, and Toner, describing an education service, recommends developing a model of service that will encourage and support young people to participate fully in its development.

Centre-based services

There is widespread agreement about the structure of such services. In general, they must be as open and accessible as possible, providing a combination of 'walk in' and appointments. They should recognise the chaotic lifestyles led by young people involved in prostitution. The requirements of young men and women may differ, and separate access to the service may be required by each gender. A welcoming, informal and non-threatening atmosphere is essential.

Meeting immediate practical needs is a vital element of an effective service. Specifically, the following should be catered to; food, laundry, washing facilities, sanitary supplies and toiletries and bus fares to attend clinics. Information is another crucial area of service provision. Young people need information on health care, social welfare, housing, childcare, alcohol and drug abuse and sexual health care. Care services should include counselling on general health, drugs and alcohol, pregnancy and contraception, HIV/AIDS and relationships and medical advice, pregnancy testing, sexual health screening, condoms and a confidential telephone service should be provided. Effective and appropriate referrals to specialised services are most important. These will include drug treatment, medical assistance and specialised counselling.

Outreach services

Toner has a developed a detailed model of outreach services comprising two elements: streetreach and an educational service. A primary characteristic of streetreach services is that children can be engaged in their own environment and facilitated to use other centre-based services. Streetreach services should:

- Operate a holistic child-centred approach.
- Identify young people not in touch with services.
- Make contact with young people who are being sexually exploited through prostitution.
- Provide materials to young people on the streets.
- Make contact with young people involved in the care system.
- Network with other organisations.

An education service has a wide remit and includes:

- Supplying information about the service to schools, GPs, community youth centres and all personnel working with young people.
- Providing training resources to schools and professionals working with young people.
- Providing professionals with skills to present information about risks of sexual exploitation and strategies to avoid this.
- Developing a model of practice that will encourage and support young people to participate fully in the development of the service.
- Developing a peer education model of practice.
- Developing a model of inclusion for adults.

Staff training

New ways of working with different client groups requires development of new skills, and a number of sources identified training as a key element of service development. Some professional staff experience difficulties in dealing with the issue of child prostitution, and this needs to be addressed. Quinlan, (1997), observes that many professionals may feel inadequate around the whole issue of sexuality.

A particular example of this is agency staff identifying the presence of young men who are open about their gay sexuality as a problem. But is it a problem for the young men concerned, for the staff, for other users of the service? Heterosexism or presumed heterosexuality by adults causes situations where a young gay person is classed as confused, where if they are heterosexual it is not questioned, but encouraged. As young people become confident about their sexuality, especially gay, lesbian and bisexuality, and therefore more visible, the agencies need to respond adequately.

A National Strategy

The previous section described a model of provision based around locally based, easily accessible services. Brief reference has been made to the need for a multi-agency approach that recognises the complexity of the issue and the fact that it cannot be seen in isolation from other social and environmental factors. However, local initiatives, whether by voluntary or statutory bodies, are usually dependent on a small number of committed individuals and so a multi-agency response is unlikely to materialise out of thin air.

Service provision nationwide will require a national response. As Toner argues:

...a national strategy should be put in place by the Department of Health for the development of services for children exploited in prostitution. This strategy plan should then be adapted by each health board to the local situation, with the aim of addressing the issue of child prostitution in the locality.

The development of a national strategy is the essential next step towards the establishment of effective prevention measures and a network of nationwide services for children involved in prostitution.

References

Barnardo's (1996). *Children on Inner City Streets in Dublin*. Barnardo's unpublished report.

Eastern Health Board (1997). *Report of Working Party on Children in Prostitution*. Eastern Health Board.

McElwee, N. and Lalor, K. (1997). *Prostitution in Waterford City—A Contemporary Analysis*. Waterford: Streetsmart Press.

O'Sullivan, M. (1998). *Prostitution in the Mid West Region*. Mid Western Health Board.

Quinlan, M. (1997). *Men in Prostitution*. Gay Men's Health Project (Eastern Health Board).

Toner, R. (1998). *Research Findings into Children at Risk in the Dundalk Area*. Youth Initiative in Partnership Project.

Chapter 5

Immigrants and Illegal Youth Sex Workers in Italy

Nicola Mullenger

The numbers of young people working in the sex trade in Italy are much disputed and difficult to corroborate. The huge influx of people moving to Italy or commuting in and out during recent years, has made the statistics both varied and vague. There is nevertheless one agreed and obvious fact, that the numbers are rising and the age is getting lower.

At the time of publishing, the findings in 1998 of the Baltic Sea States Summit, which took place in Riga, estimated that 30 per cent of the prostitutes in Western Europe are young people, ranging from 12 to 18 years, coming mainly from the Eastern parts of the continent. Whilst Italy is only a part of Western Europe, its traditional involvement in organised crime combined with emergent illegal groups originating outside of Italy, has leapt upon these young people and developed a strong trade. This chapter concentrates on this phenomena of mass immigration and traffic into Italy from Central and Eastern European Countries, and, additionally looks at the smaller numbers of young people from Asia and Africa and the organisations that have emerged to support them.

Recently, people of all ages and both sexes have been entering Italy without legal documents. Unfortunately, Italy is a country that does not have an established infrastructure for dealing with the arrival of such quantities of 'foreigners'. In this context, foreign describes the term of not permanently residing in the country and not necessarily with the intention of a permanent stay; it is also used by society to alienate persons who have a legal right to live in the particular country. The general impact has been fed by the classic media hype, heightened by their physical visibility, and about increasing crime. In the last ten years, the steady increase of immigrants has predominantly included communities from Asia, North Africa and Eastern and Central

European countries. This has escalated into a declared emergency within Italy and now includes people from the former Soviet Union and wider Africa. This 'utopian' hot spot has never experienced anything similar.

Nationality Diversity

In the 1970s, Italy was usually the source of numerous emigrants and only began attracting immigrants when the traditional labour importing countries of Europe put a stop to the recruitment of foreign labour. During the 1980s, Italy became a destination for significant numbers of migrants from developing countries. Despite the period of time that Italy had to prepare itself by introducing policies that could ease the admission pains of the immigrant worker, 'the migration occurred largely at the margin of the law', (Barsotti and Lecchini). In the early 1980s many migrants became guests of Italy naturally and without documentation. During the late 1980s, to cope with the rapid development, migration controls were set in place. These focused on non-European Community peoples and were finally adopted in 1986 and 1990. It was commonly known as the Martelli Law, (n. 39 of 28 February 1990, and Article 7 discusses the expulsion of clandestine immigrants). To catch up with all the previous, undocumented persons who had already migrated to Italy, the government set about, among other things, regularisation drives. Some 105,000 and later 216,00 'foreigners' became 'regularised', (EURIPIES Scheda 50). A breakdown of nationalities showed 23 per cent were North African, 12 per cent sub-Saharan and African and 18 per cent from Asia, accounting for 53 per cent of the newly registered immigrants.

However, this does not mean to say all immigrants are working in the sex industry, nor involved in microcriminalità, that is, crimes of theft, burglary, sexual assault and mugging, but the illegal status of many living in Italy has limited their employment possibilities, and public reaction has seized on the link between the flood of immigrants and rising crime figures.

Since these findings, further research, (Da Pra, 1999), has been undertaken on the public reaction to immigrants, their integration within Italy, the arrival of various age groups, deciphering links with criminality and the levels of applications for visa permits. Again, in 1997, a decree was passed to 'discipline the wave of immigration on the social condition', (Ministero dell'Interno, 1998), and increased the documentation needed to apply for a visa. At the end of 1998, it was considered necessary to revise the entries into the country. The new immigration legislation, which remains valid until 2000, concentrates on balancing the needs of estimated labour by the Ministry of

Work and by the Social Security Ministry. Interestingly, the decree has acknowledged the demand from specific nationalities and allowed a limited number of visas to be issued on condition of relevant documents regarding proof of address and labour contracts, directly to Albania, Morocco and Tunisia. These visas can be granted prior to entrance to Italy by the governments of these countries. However, one condition is that all previous visa holders by 27th March, 1998 have priority if they still are in receipt of labour and housing contracts. Therefore the number of permits given to a new selection of applications is smaller. Despite the ratification from the Italian Government of commitment to migrants, these yearly revisions clearly do not directly apply to all young people who arrive, most of whom are illegally trafficked. The main method of entry is by using a three month tourist visa, and then staying on after its expiry. This is normally administered by an illegal group who charge the cost of these false papers to the girl, and hence named 'debt bondage', (Bindman and Doezema, 1997). Another method is to use a university visa, frequently granted to the infamous 'boyfriend' who then can just apply for a friend to accompany him, so long as he is providing hospitality. Not all the traffickers are male, for example the Nigerian, 'La Grande Maman', (La Stampa, 10th February, 1996). These groups organise the movement, exchange of papers and persons by means of several 'hired helpers'. One of the difficulties in challenging traffickers is the silent chain structure which separates the individuals, who only perform their own designated tasks. Therefore, the young person normally only has contact with the individual 'sender' in the country of origin, and the individual 'receiver' in the country of destination.

Overview of Legal History

There has been a continual exposure of youth sex crimes in Italy, which have been noted by the statistical groups such as Census, who reported:

> *...that the prostitution of Albanian youth from 14 upwards can be defined as a particularly dramatic problem...It is an emergency, because the phenomenon of the exploitation has expanded and doesn't have a foreseeable break...*

> (*La Repubblica*, 16 July, 1998)

The obvious impracticality of re-opening brothels, closed by the Merlin Law in 1958, to monitor the workers has forced parliament to review new legislation under different titles; all have been denied. The Merlin Law was introduced after much pressure from Lina Merlin and the neighbouring countries of Italy, who, along with France all adopted the abolitionist stance that conformed with international resolutions issued first by the League of Nations and later by the United Nations. The Merlin Law effectively closed all existing brothels and banned any sort of direct or indirect registration and the medical examinations of prostitutes. The term 'aiding and abetting' came into use, whereby working from the streets or cohabiting with another prostitute theoretically would bring punishment from the law.

To compensate for the sudden lack of brothel employment, the state committed itself to establishing reformatories for both youth and adults and introduced a female police force to take responsibility for public concern and youth prostitution. Needless to say, neither were really given the force and economic backing to continue to function, (Gibson, 1986).

An inter-ministerial co-ordination group was set up in April, 1998, between the Italian and the United States governments. It is described in the International Organisation of Migration quarterly bulletin (www.iom.int) as a 'working group on trafficking in women and children, and was created as a result of the consultations with the respective Foreign Ministers', (IOM Trafficking Bulletin, June, 1998). The over-riding aims are for 'the safe return of victims, and appropriate arrangements for temporary or permanent legal status for victims and witnesses'. This task involves a long-term commitment requiring massive resources, and the constant attention and determination of the political policy makers.

New Legislation for a Visa

In January, 1999, the political policy makers, Pia Covre, Laura Balbo, (Ministry of Equal Opportunity), Livia Turco, (Ministry of Social Solidarity), and Maria Rosa Jervolino, (Ministry of Internal Affairs), created a visa for the women who are 'slave sex workers', (*La Repubblica*, 27 January, 1999), and are forced to work in the sex industry. This new legislation has been formally passed and could provide an exit from the trafficker/pimp regime for the women who want to leave.

A 'green line', (a freephone number), has been promised for women and young people to call for referral to a relevant organisation that will help them, although this is not yet operational. This seems to be setting up the mechanism whereby, according to the legislation, the women and young people can inform an organisation of their existence and situation, instead of talking directly to the police as was previously the case. The three women, Balbo, Turco and Jervolino insist that to succeed in weakening the hold of the traffickers, the 'exploited' must be provided with a viable alternative, namely the professional expertise of an organisation with the experience of 'at least working in the field for three years' and who are local to the women and young people.

Caritas, Gruppo Abele and Giovanni XXIII are some of the nationwide organisations who stress the importance that the programme be open without the prerequisite of collaborating with the police for information on traffickers. These organisations have been working for many years towards the safety of trafficked young people at local levels, with the municipal and social services assisting with the processing of the visa. In turn, the legislation allows for longer punishment terms for the traffickers, increasing the sentence of imprisonment for promoting clandestine prostitution from five to fifteen years. Thus, it is hoped the traders are not released, as previously, after serving only very short sentences. The increased severity of the measures towards the trafficker may indicate a further commitment to the traded young sex worker. It is hoped these changes in the law could bring a more positive involvement for young people in deciding their future.

The legalisation, however, declares that the organisation still cannot administer the visa and the young people will have to be in direct contact with the police. As mentioned earlier, according to several organisations in Italy, contact was specifically not wanted with the police, due to the nervous reaction of the young people. Although they are surrendering an often painful and limited existence, the alternative of returning to a country that may be poorly structured, both economically and socially, only offers them an equally disdainful option, and one which may not necessarily provide a positive resolution either.

An earlier protection programme was created by the government and administered by the Italian police, who say 'killings of women forced into prostitution average one a month', (Spector, 11 January, 1998). According to the immigration specialist Daniela Pompei only twenty women used it. She works with the community of Sant'Egidio, a Catholic relief agency in Rome, and notes, 'The police is the last place these women want to go'. Thus, the visa and contact with the police should be handled with caution.

Another concern lies with the possible quantities of youth and sex traded workers applying for the visa, as the percentage of 'foreign' prostitutes working are far greater than Italian nationals.

> ...the EC divider between citizens of the European Community and foreigners is fallacious since southern citizens, from Greece, Italy, Spain or Portugal, are likely to face greater discrimination than 'white' non-EC people from richer countries such as the United States and Australia.
> (Pheterson, 1996: p 153)

The problem is the regulation of employment and provision of work for the young people and other visa holders, as Italy has an established predicament of employment shortages for its present national citizens.

Once again, it is noted by officials, like Balbo, that most of the criminal organisations are based outside Italy. She cites an article, entitled 'Welcome to Milan, Italy's Wild West', and which states 'foreign gangs, in particular Albanians and Slavic groups, control prostitution in Milan, and much of the drug trade', (Kennedy, *The Independent*, 17th January, 1999) (*La Repubblica*, 27th January, 1999). A reinforced co-operation with other countries is needed in order to have the funding, professionals and structures to face the problem of trafficking at an international level. It is clear that the Italian Government feel they have satisfied a need that has been shown frequently by analysis from International, European and nationwide committees, organisations, parliament members, specialists and volunteers. However, the cry is for international support and this is vital, since without this, communication and action will suffer and in effect, the work needed delayed. As Mikhail Lebed, Chief of Criminal Investigations for the Ukrainian Interior Ministry says:

> *We have a very serious problem here, and we are simply not equipped to solve it by ourselves. It is a human tragedy, but also frankly a national crisis. Gangsters make more from these women in a week than we have in our law-enforcement budget for the whole year. To be honest, unless we get some help we are not going to stop it.*

> (Spector, 1998)

A report made by The Committee on Civil Liberties and Internal Affairs of the European Parliament in 1993 said, that 'raising barriers around the European Union is unrealistic'. Claudia Roth goes on to say:

> *It must be assumed that both refugees and people in search of better living conditions will continue their efforts to settle in the European Union in the future, possibly in greater numbers...faced with this situation the European Union must not become a fortress...we should moreover, pursue a policy that tackles the causes of migration...*

> (Wijers and Lap-Chew, 1996: p 147)

Several routes have been identified as being used for recurrent trafficking of immigrants: one named the 'Sea Route' by the Austrian authorities goes through Greece and Italy, (IOM, 1998). Another example we hear of is the boat journey from Albania to Italy, often landing in the province of Brindisi; this has the reputation as a very dangerous passage, as reported in the distressing bulletins of very young children being thrown overboard to prevent capsizing, (Panorama, 22 October, 1998), and (Ruggiero, 1997).

> *...too many Albanians minors get into the web of criminal gangs who bring them to the street after giving them the illusion of finding them a place to live in Italy. It happened to this fifteen year old. Some of these acquaintances had promised her a job and marriage.*
>
> (*La Repubblica*, 19th January, 1999).

> *The trafficking in Albanians is rife in the South of Italy. There is only a narrow strait separating Albania from the coast of the region of Puglia. Here the coastguard patrol is particularly severe, as dozens of small boats illegally carry Albanians into the Italian territory*
>
> (Ruggiero, 1997: p 5)[13]

Provincial Agendas

In the last three years, Italy has started to research the immigrants' state of origin and the 'hosted' country, to understand the structure of immigration. As with anything that happens constantly and quickly, the social, political and public reactions have been slow to become informed of measures to better the situation. Each province in Italy has been concerned about the increase of sexual crime, which includes abuse within the term microcriminalità, and especially as each area has a differing agenda. Large cities in the north such as Milan, Turin, Venice and Genoa link these figures with a steady growth of youth immigrants involved or subjected to sexual violence, selling drugs and paedophilia, whilst Brescia in the north records an increase of obligated immigrant prostitution. In the south, Rome has seen a rise of sexual crime and Lecce and Catania speak of a huge youth involvement with Mafia and other illegal criminal organisations. In the central areas, Florence warns of massive arrivals constituting the formation of a real criminal organisation. Bologna is waiting for a new reform to make the justice system more efficient as killings linked with sexual abuse are intensifying, (*La Repubblica*, 11th January, 1999).

Unless projects orchestrated by organisations are made directly available to the young people, then contact is improbable. When the free phone green line has been set up, it will be interesting to see how many will use it. Fear of returning to the country of citizenship is real. Pino Gulia, representing Caritas, explains, 'theirs are extreme situations...in this reality of continuous violence, danger and blackmail', (*La Repubblica*, 21st January, 1999). Both possibilities are damaging; either to return home or to leave the racket's protection. It will involve courage from the young person to pursue the possibility promised by the new legislation for visas. The trust given by them will rest in the effectiveness of the police co-operation with existing organisations, which they may already have had contact with on the street.

It is noticeable that these organisations filled the vacuum that arose from the unkempt support networks promised by the Merlin Law and throughout the years reacted to the change of demography of the prostitute working in Italy. These programmes started to educate the public by liaising with traditional Catholic opinions and masculine oriented ethics, re-highlighting the problem of child labour, discussing the present identity and status of the prostitute and providing invaluable support and practical help to young people at ground level.

These organisations are the public's and politician's main source of information on the identity of the traded sex worker. As when mediating, the transformation from self managed prostitution (10 per cent), to foreign, normally exploited workers (90 per cent), the real issues are of clandestine prostitution working for food, or because they are obligated by the 'racket', (*La Repubblica*, 22nd August, 1999). Thus, an understanding of non-choice in the sex worker's role has had to be put forward repeatedly to all citizens.

National Based Organisations Referred to by International Centres

Comitato per i Diritti Civili delle Prostitute was founded in 1982, co-ordinated by and working for the rights of sex workers. Carla Corso and Pia Covre have been well documented through their work with Comitato, which has formed a part of LILA (Lega Italiana per la contro i'AIDS/ Italian League to Struggle against AIDS). The Comitato also forms a part of EUROCASO (European Council of AIDS Service Organisations). The Comitato was formed 'in response to continued violence at the hands of American soldiers at the NATO base at Aviano and the failure of the Italian police to protect them from it...', (Gibson, 1986). In 1983, it organised a national convention and produced its own newspaper named 'lucciola' (firefly—the colloquial expression for street-workers). This organisation provides nation wide support to sex workers in the community and includes education for the general public, specifically in AIDS prevention programmes (LILA). In 1993, collaborated work with TAMPEP, (Transnational STD/AIDS Prevention Among Migrant Prostitutes in the European Union) started in several areas of Italy. TAMPEP selected Comitato through the 'willingness to embrace the needs of migrant sex workers'.

Reportedly, 'both statutory and non-governmental agencies active in the Italian AIDS field have been generally reluctant to address this area and do not consider it a priority', (TAMPEP final report, 1994: p 109).

The context of the HIV epidemic in Europe, shows that the Southern nations are by far those most affected: 72 per cent of AIDS diagnoses in Europe were reported in three Mediterranean countries, France, Italy and Spain. Consequently, health services becoming available to non-EC communities have been difficult to establish, with the concern to firstly look after the Italians. It was noted in the report of the collaboration between TAMPEP and Comitato, that the 'clandestine migrant' operation happening in Italy, appears prominent in relation to other countries, Germany and The Netherlands, in which TAMPEP was involved. Despite this obstacle, informative material, translated into Albanian, Romanian, Italian and English was successfully distributed to other young people by the group of traded sex workers initially contacted. Needless to say, the uncertainty of Italian immigration policy has hindered the decisions of health staff and state run faculties, which has not been helped by the difficult and cumbersome paperwork needed to allow treatment. This, in turn, has driven the sex worker underground.

One of the programmes Comitato has dedicated itself to is the provision of health care vans, operating for young people working on the street. Since 1993, financed primarily by the Health Ministry and now the European Union community, Comitato has had street vans in Venice, Novara, Turin and Emilia Romagna, the region where Bologna is located. This permanent sight of support allows the young people to have some health care treatment, which would otherwise be unavailable through fear of reprisals from pimps or arousing interest from the authorities. In regional organisations, communication between project workers and hospitals has allowed a considerable number of women to be treated with minimal legal concerns.

Comitato is seen as a mediator between sex workers and the legal instruments of Italy. One example, in 1996, apart from the constant referencing and acknowledgements in European reports of projects, Comitato liaised between sex workers in Riccione and its local municipal authorities. This area is noted as an extremely busy seaside resort; the sea road provides an ideal platform to work and the local residents and public started to increase the pressure to 'clean-up' the road. Dom. Oresta Benzi, who founded Papa Giovanni XXIII, (a Catholic organisation that provides help to the spiritually enlightened sex traded workers), published shock initiatives in the Catholic newspaper *Avvenire*, telling of the 'crisis' in Riccione. The Mayor of Riccione relied on the cultural mediation of Comitato to move the women to another part of the city.

Projects Connected with Nationally Based Organisations Within Europe

TAMPEP, along with Comitato, is a partner in a European based project including Amsterdam and Hamburg, working with 'clandestine migrants' throughout Italy. Namely, Nigerian sex workers in Turin, South American sex workers in Milan, Eastern European sex workers in Bologna, Verona, Pordenone and Latin Americans also from Pordenone. It is difficult to specify the number of sex traded workers who were young people, due to the lack of precise information given by the worker, but the figures undoubtedly do include this group.

The central aim of the project was providing education on the prevention of sexually transmitted diseases and, during 1996 and 1997, TAMPEP linked schemes with EUROPAP, an intervention project. Many of the workers they contacted had come from countries where sex is not spoken of openly and preventative measures are not easily available. Included in this is the spiritual idea of infertility and bad magic 'voodoo', connected with use of contraception, especially amongst the Nigerian community. This officially European funded programme communicated to the traded sex worker, the public and politicians alike the need for such work, especially with non-national or non-European Community peoples.

The recommendations strengthened several arguments, including, for example, self empowerment through personal health care and the encouragement of condom usage, whilst at the same time emphasising the necessity to continue supporting organisations dedicated to these peoples.

European Projects Connecting National Based Organisations

EUROPAP, the European Intervention Project's AIDS prevention for prostitutes, aims to work with existing organisations and local municipality administrations that are eager to implement non-repressive interventions that strive towards creating projects for the prevention of AIDS/STDs amongst prostitutes. The local co-ordinators were Pia Covre from Comitato per i Diritti Civili delle Prostitute and Dr Vittono Agnoletto and Paolo La Marca from Lega Italiana per la lotta contro i AIDS.

Further understanding was achieved by holding a press conference and organising meetings in Milan, Rome and Bologna. In Milan, September 1995, a city meeting, 'Hunt for the Fireflies', was organised which emphasised the enterprise of some municipalities in using scare tactics to counter prostitution. 'Closing some streets to traffic in the evening, confiscation of cars as 'evidence', big police raids and so on', (Mak, 1996). It gave the opportunity for the press, media, politicians and local town groups complaining of the 'plague' of prostitution, to meet with organisations and discuss the real issues surrounding the subject of health care for sex workers. EUROPAP stressed the 'very fabric of Italian culture is strongly Catholic and tends to be extremely moralistic'.

A list of recommendations were collated, based upon the premise that in Italy, prostitutes and sex traded workers continue to suffer a heavy social stigma originating from the dominant moral values of the 'temporary' residing country. Thus, in line with the World Health Organisation resolutions, continuing schemes for active prevention, and education were implemented. The work and report subsequently produced by Mak in 1996 brought together the social, ethical, and cultural values in Italy when describing the climate for education and information projects aimed at sex workers. A concern for creating a link between organisations, whether new or established, is voiced and included in many other European reports, (TAMPEP, EUROPAP, ECPAT 1996).

In 1996 the Ministry of Health in Italy did not approve a parliamentary bill suggesting mandatory screening for HIV and concluded that prevention orientated ways of intervention seemed to be a better endorsement and in the long-term, more successful. Some of the campaigns by EUROPAP involve 'outreach' programmes, including giving condoms and sterile needles on an exchange basis. The integration of public and non-public bodies, enabled professional members of the community and experts in volunteer organisations to work together with the use of public funds. A self empowerment attitude is promoted towards the use of the health care system along with the individual's own personal health care. Automatic access for immigrants to free health care is needed; presently they need to be hospitalised in order to receive treatment, unless local organisations mediate on their behalf. Finally, the repressive laws on illegal clandestine workers need modifying to allow the work done by organisations to be more effective in containing the spread of HIV.

National Based Organisations

The Papa Giovanni XXIII is a well known organisation that is very useful in its engagement of the general public in Italy, because of the organisation's religious structure. However, its questionable ethics of conversion to faith, before women are self empowered and helped practically, (i.e. accommodation), encourages doubts of its effectiveness.

The Caritas organisation does not work on the street, but by referral system from the Questura, Local Council and even clients. It has European projects and works directly to prevent trafficking and slavery. Unlike Giovanni XXIII, the women and men are not obliged to become Catholic or in the case of Caritas, not Christian.

Gruppo Abele deals with many cases of social 'outcasts' such as AIDS patients, alcoholics, prostitutes, people with immigration problems, and sufferers from Mafia criminality. It started with the needs of street work in the 1970s and developed its existing programmes using an organic, 'bottom up growth', approach. It is funded by members contributions and raises money by events and information services such as CD-ROMs. The organisation has many connections, both within and outside Europe, and disseminates information on film, by dissertations, newspaper articles both national and international, and through its own Gruppo Abele periodical. It has material for schools, libraries, universities, social assistants, professionals in general, ministries, and youth and voluntary organisations.

The direct help for sex workers from Gruppo Abele is via street vans or units. They also run a hospitality programme on a three month or one year residency basis, which aims to provide a close relationship between the 'guest' and 'host'. At the same, time individual freedom is respected, with a direct focus on autonomy as a result. Hostel places are offered, which depend on the need of the individual, with donations available from Gruppo Abele. With the work from both communities, hospitality is given to 170 people each year on short term (three month), or long term (12 month) programmes for AIDS sufferers, young mothers and others with long term needs. The organisation deals with a wide range of people who need support, and has a strong network involved in hospitality programmes within the community of Turin, where it is based. The organisation does not directly focus on the requirements of the girls, due to a wide range of needs that Gruppo Abele works with, but the individual circumstance of the young traded sex worker can still receive support.

Provincial Based Organisation

The organisation Mimosa started in February, 1996 as a voluntary group, who recognised that in Tencarola, a province surrounding Padova near Venice, many young women arrived through the commercial market of the sex trade industry. Since then, the members of the organisation have been actively working towards providing a structure of support to the workers, both on education and health care. By November, 1998, about 450 traded sex workers had contacted Mimosa via the 'outreach' programme, aged between 13 and

26. The Mimosa volunteers, who regularly meet the workers through the night by driving around and stopping to speak with them, found that by deducting two years from the workers self-stated age they got a more accurate figure. Mimosa affirms a permanent link with the Albanians, with increasing numbers of Romanians from 1997, with new contacts from the former Soviet Union communities towards the end of 1998, whilst at the same time keeping up a constant interaction with Africans and Latin Americans.

This organisation aims to give groundwork support on health, prevention, information about legal help, physiological needs, housing problems and access to health care. Since 1997, with the permanent co-operation of the SERT of the USSL (the local state run health services), Mimosa secured medical equipment for specific health checks and blood analysis exclusively for the sex workers on the street or residing in the organisation's accommodation.

It is the organisation's belief that, for these women and young people, there is no guarantee of their rights, especially concerning the proposed opening of 'brothels' or by creating 'red light districts'. This is likely to cause a barrier to the social reality and hide the existence of sex traded sex workers. The demand from clients is increasing, therefore a developing trade for sex workers of different ages and nationalities is created, simply because there is a 'requirement'. Mimosa also noted:

> *we have recently registered growing demand from the young workers, therefore if red light districts and brothels should use this…[method of workplace]…this would become inhuman exploitation.*

(Mimosa, 1998)

They conclude the discussion of specially designated places to sell sex as, 'not facing the social reality and consequently offering false expectations'.

The aim of Mimosa is to promote the individual's personal autonomy. Designated spaces run by hierarchical structures, whether they be government organisations or illegal trading groups, would not improve the situation for illegal sex traded workers.

The volunteer needs to avoid giving confrontational advice to sex workers, as the whole basis of their relationship is friendship and unconditional help. With the use of a human reference point, the young person can feel more in control, albeit the amount of control is small in reality. There is still little monitoring of the situation conducted at local or national level, even though it has been compared to Thailand in certain areas of the country.

> *Alarm: Increasing Youth Prostitution, Italy has become like Thailand, and you cannot close your eyes and think that the exploitation is a far*

away problem. Following the statistics, many prostitutes in Italy are under twelve and youth immigrants from Eastern Europe, Nigeria and Africa in general and most of them are from Albania. This is an evaluation from CENSUS.

(La Repubblica, 16th July, 1998)

Venice and its surrounding areas funnel the traffic from the north, from Slovenia through Trieste and from Eastern and Central Europe. Venice, Mestre, Padova and Brescia lead in turn to Milan, which is currently defending its name as the fashion capital, not the crime capital, of Italy, (*The Independent*, 17th January, 1999). The main problem is one of inadequate statistics about the young people and where they travel. Many told of staying in Milan for the weekend at the direction of their pimp. Since, the World Sex Guide on the Internet—now often blocked by servers—publicised the correct newspaper and provides translations of certain expressions, for the travelling businessman etc. who frequently stays in Milan with sex in mind. Sex workers, who quoted their ages as eighteen, spoke of working in Rome or Turin for a while, and many talked about going on to live in other areas of Europe such as Germany or the Netherlands. Thus, with such rapid and spontaneous movement, it is difficult to 'reunite' worker and volunteer. Mimosa works hard for contact with other similar organisations to strengthen action, on both a regional and national basis, and, given the sporadic movement between cities and countries, this is a crucial part of their success.

One of the main projects co-ordinated by Mimosa is a 'hospitality' arrangement that aims to provide the personal growth, autonomy, and self-awareness for the young people to fight the 'racket'. It does not exclude women with children, those without a visa or those with HIV. The organisation proposes that the safe house has the characteristics of support in a trustful environment and can provide education, such as language tuition, psychological support and professional training. Mimosa also suggests that without co-operation from the traded workers, the police intervention is less efficient in arresting the criminals. Generally, this co-operation is unlikely since they will have no accommodation apart from that which is organised by the trafficker who 'administers' their earnings, but Mimosa has been able to obtain visas for some thirty young women, along with six of their children. A number of these young women have been able to give information to the police in cases involving prostitution trafficking, exploitation, physical and sexual violence and murders.

This illustrates some of the work Mimosa has achieved through the contacts and connections of local families, church figures, and youth associations, and the Papa Giovanni XXIII organisation. After consulting and sharing experience and know-how, Caritas and Association Congress in January, 1998, decided upon the approved function of a safe house which opened in March, 1999, with the aim of supporting young people over periods of 6–8 months. Other links with TAMPEP have succeeded in distributing translated material, organising private and public health care for sex workers and the long-term analysis of preventative education strategies.

Padova is experiencing a rising tide of youth prostitution, including a demand for girls below the age of consent. There are about a hundred of these under age girls working on the streets and 'in some waves of arrivals there are as many as two hundred', (Mimosa, October 1998). The realistic approach is to provide street units on the ground; however, obtaining funding remains problematic. The FarRETE project work, based on the 285 Law, deals especially with the young. This intervention aims to contact the under 18s by using the mobile van type strategy. Despite this move to contact working young people on the street, in reality more and more of the young people are working inside clubs or houses, and protecting them becomes extremely difficult.

When working with the young women during the night, Laura, an Albanian who travelled to Italy, as her sister had done previously, said 'there was nothing left for me there'. She asked why people would be interested in knowing about her life and about others in this situation. The general ambivalence of the police, organisations, traffickers and politicians make the individual traded worker certainly suspicious. In order to provide assistance an organisation not only has to find the sex traded worker, but also needs to establish a starting point of trust.

Conclusions

We have seen throughout the Western hemisphere that the cases of youth prostitution do not solely rely on migration or mass social or economic poverty from another continent. It happens daily, within reach of the urban centres and rural settings of the developed 'sophisticated' countries with which we are familiar.

Article 18 of the new immigration law introduced in February, 1999, may help to provide some status, both ethically and legally, for 'foreign' women and young people. As the young sex trade worker does not feel, nor have identity in many cases with the term prostitute, self-protection is difficult. Without an understanding of sexually transmitted diseases and birth control for example, prevention of further dangers is near impossible. Prostitution can be a profession, but these young people are not professional. They learn of the street dangers, but are still often left exposed due to their lack of situational control. Only if they are lucky will they receive information from assisting organisations.

The general public will continue to exert pressure from the increase in crime and its links with 'deviants' and migrants. In Italy, there is a need for a general raising of cultural awareness and equality issues. Simultaneously, the Italian Federation of Travel and Tourism Associations and Enterprises has recommended to its members that they should combat sex tourism. As a result of the agreement with ECPAT Italy, a brochure to warn tourists against sexual exploitation of young people will be handed out.

Further communication and long-term support networks are needed to link Italy and Western Europe with socially, economically and politically developing countries particularly regarding young people and the protection of their rights. 'On the Road', an anti-trafficking organisation in central Italy (Teramo), noted the differing demands of clients; paler Eastern European women commanded a higher price than the Nigerians and Asians. However, 'Ukrainians have reduced their 'income' as the influx of women has grown gradually, to the extent that the other women of different nationalities complain', (Personal correspondence, July, 1999). This trend is confirmed by Mimosa who has noticed the other former Soviet Union communities arriving to work in Italy.

It is a matter of survival on the street and no matter what legislative controls are put in place the traffickers and the drug rackets continue to change in order to make more money with no regard for their responsibilities. The movement of young women through different hands in the present day is greater than ever before. Today, the young continue to be sold after answering adverts in newspapers or being 'removed' from their homes and appear to change overnight. If they manage to get out of the system either by finally returning to their country or by denouncing their protector, the task of adapting to their former life is complex. The Albanians that Mimosa supports in their house want the freedom to disassociate themselves from their country.

The strain and trauma associated with youth sex work are varied and include prejudice, economics and cultural conflict. Many of the foreign young sex workers in Italy find they are in an invidious situation. If they stay in Italy they have no papers, are stateless and at the mercy of the criminals. If they return to their country of origin, they struggle with a cultural and identity crisis. Irrespective of origin, its an unenviable position to be in.

References

Balbo, L. (1999). In *La Repubblica*, 27th January (Ministry of Equal Opportunity).

Baltic Sea States (1998). Summit, *Commercial Sexual Exploitation of Children in the Baltic Sea Region*, Doc. Dk-98/62.

Barsotti, O. and Lecchini, L. (1995). *The Experience of Filipino Female Migrants in Italy.* (Publisher).

Bindman, J., and Doezema, J. (1997). *Redefining Prostitution as Sex Work on the International Agenda.* London: Anti Slavery International.

Da Pra, M. (1999). *Il ruolo ed il rapporto con i mezzi di informazione nel campo dalle prostituzione e della tratta*, 26th March, 1999.

Gibson, M. (1986). *Prostitution and the State in Italy 1860–1915.* New Brunswick: Rutgers University Press.

La Stampa (1996). *La Grande Maman*, (article) 10th February, 1996.

Pheterson, G. (1996). *The Prostitution Prism.* Amsterdam Press.

Ruggiero, V. (1997). *Trafficking in Human Beings: Slaves in Europe.* London: Middlesex University.

Spector, M. (1998). *Traffickers New Cargo: Naïve Slav Women*, (article) www.captive.org/articleseasteurope.htm, 11th January, 1998.

Wijers, M., and Lap-Chew, L. (1997). Trafficking in Women, Forced Labour and Slavery-like Practices in Marriage, *Domestic Labour and Prostitution.* Utrecht: STV.

Organisations

Caritas
Comitato Comitato per i Diritti Ciuilli delle Prostitute
ECPAT The International Campaign to End Child Prostitution in Asian Tourism
EURIPIES
EUROCASO European Council of AIDS Service Organisations
EUROPAP European Intervention Project's AIDS Prevention for Prostitution
Gruppo Abele
IOM International Organisation of Migration (www.iom.int)
LILA Italian League to Struggle Against AIDS
Mimosa
Papa Giovanni XXIII
TAMPEP Transnational STD/AIDS Prevention Amongst Migrant Prostitutes in the European
   Union

Chapter 6

Young People and Sex Work in the Netherlands

David Barrett

Introduction

In 1993, the Council of Europe published *Sexual Exploitation, Pornography and the Prostitution of and Trafficking in Children and Young Persons*. The report observes that if child and teenage prostitution is to be prevented, there is a need for mobile units of social workers who would target particularly vulnerable groups who are seen to be easy prey to pimps and other recruiting agents. These are seen to be 'emotionally damaged children from broken homes, runaways, drug addicts and street children'. The report suggested that there should be continuous control of places which are likely to attract young prostitutes and their clients like central railway stations, airports and seaports. The central railway station in Amsterdam attracted young prostitutes in 1993, it still does now and is likely to for some time to come.

Seeing a group of young people waiting stoically for 'their' support agency to open, usually in the mid to late afternoon, brings home the sad reality that socially deprived, abused and disadvantaged young people look remarkably similar whether they are standing in a street in Amsterdam, Paris or London. So, too, is the fact that such deprivation is concentrated amongst particular social classes and racial groups. Thus the disproportionate involvement of Irish and Moroccan young people in male prostitution in London is paralleled by the involvement of Moroccans and Surinamese young people in Amsterdam. The representation of young Muslim women in prostitution in Amsterdam is, according to *Stichting Streetcornerwork*, often a product of cultural conflict between parents and children which leads to ejection from home and consequent homelessness. These are matters that one of the practice based agencies that specialise in services for young people in the sex industry know well, *Stichting Streetcornerwork*, (1999). As many commentators have noted, above all else, it is economic factors which propel young people into the sex industry, (Van der Ploeg, 1989; O'Neill, 1991; Barrett, 1994).

This chapter is perhaps more reflective than the others, it has considerable material to contemplate not least because the degree to which the sex industry in the Netherlands is both well established and embedded in the culture of the country. This is an internal and external perception. Political, ideological and empirical material is explored. There is more mention of 'boys' too because, at its simplest, the denial associated with boys and the sex industry that is prevalent in other European countries, is minimal. The majority of the chapter however considers developed and sophisticated harm reduction interventionist strategies and models of practice—they are taken primarily from Dutch publications, some are quoted at length or in full with due acknowledgements. To precis or change such material runs the risk of losing the spirit or essence. The chapter concludes with some comments about this more liberal approach to youth sex workers.

A Politicised Area of Work

Like other areas of Europe, working with young people in the sex industry remains as politicised as ever. Similar to the young people themselves, services to youngsters engaged in the sex industry are perceived as marginal, the work tends to attract those with a strong philosophical or political commitment who locate themselves as advocates for their clients. This has been the case for many years in the Netherlands. Ten years ago the following excerpt appeared in the *Vena Newsletter*:

> ...*how many women are involved in sex and marriage trafficking each year? Where do they come from and where do they go? Who are the women who are trafficked, how did they get involved? What are the best ways to prevent women from becoming victimized? How can they be supported once they are trafficked? And last but not least, how do women experience the fact that they are trafficked and work in the international sex-industry*...

These questions, a decade later, can rightly now be applied to young people's involvement in the Dutch sex industry. If anything, it has increased its significance as the epicentre of the sex industry in North West Europe.

In the municipalities of The Hague, Rotterdam and Amsterdam, the highest number of sex workers within the visible area of window prostitution are migrant women of Latin America and the Caribbean. Their presence relates to the existence of an organised sex industry in the Netherlands; the stereotyped images of women from these regions as exotic, submissive, mysterious, etc. recreated by the sex industry; the economic crisis in the 'Third World' and the feminisation of poverty; and the search for better living alternatives. The numbers of young people from countries such as Morocco, Surinam, the Antilles, and more recently Somalia, are an interesting parallel development

The lack of representation of migrant youth in debates, policies and organisations of prostitution can be seen as evidence of the marginality of their position, for example, there is no formal organisational base which represents the interests of this group such as that which exists for the Dutch prostitute (De Rode Draad/The Red Thread). Furthermore, since this group of prostitutes have been defined as a homogenous group within policies, that is, as victims of trafficking only, their needs and interests have both been unrecognised and unaccounted for.

Boys 'In de Bisnis' (primarily from Van der Poel, 1991)

In scholarly writings of those commentators like Van der Poel, (1991), and others, male prostitution is generally viewed as a multiproblematic phenomenon. The emphasis is on the period which precedes the youth's first introduction to male prostitution and on discovering solutions to the psychosocial problems generated by the phenomenon. Although most authors on the topic assume a common understanding of what is meant by male prostitution, Van der Poel argues that in reality male prostitution is a collective for a variety of totally distinct 'cash nexus' activities. Although Van der Poel's analysis is based around fieldwork from the mid 1980s, and its emphasis is on young professional sex workers, the typology remains controversial and prone to change over time. He classifies young male prostitutes on the basis of their forms of organisation and the kinds of transactions they are engaged in and four different groups of prostitutes emerge.

1. Rough trade: youths who pretend to be prostitutes but use this cover as a means to other ends: blackmail, robbery and 'gay bashing'. These youngsters are primarily delinquents who are after homosexual men. They are members of gangs and cliques.

2. Street hustlers: youths characterized by their attempts at survival on a day to day basis. They roam the inner city looking for the possibilities to lay their hands on money. They do not specialise in one specific activity, but they have several sources of income, one of which is prostitution.

3. Part-time prostitutes: youths who incidentally and individually enter the prostitution market. They are still at school or university and try to make some extra money; or they are unemployed and in this way complement their social security benefit or they have jobs and want some money to add to their salary.

4. Professional prostitutes: youths who are accepted members of the prostitution world. They consider themselves to be committed to the occupation as a career. In most cases it has been their only or a very important and regular source of income for years. Within this 'social world' it is seen to that rules of conduct are strictly abided by. The essence of these rules is the youth's reliability towards the customers as well as colleagues, which means that the prostitute warns colleagues about unreliable customers and that with customers he sticks to the conditions agreed upon when making the deal. It is a 'social world' in its own right with its own norms, values and social control techniques that are used to protect the market against the invasion of rough trade, street hustlers and part-time prostitutes.

When we look at it this way, the professional prostitutes form the core of male prostitution, whereas the other three categories are just marginal phenomena. Nonetheless, the professional prostitutes usually remain unobserved, while most of the attention is paid to the rough trade and the street hustlers to whom prostitution is either a pretext or a survival strategy. These are the troublemakers, Van der Poel argues, and like the part-time prostitutes they are operating in the margins of the prostitution world. Their activities usually deserve the name of prostitution. They are amateurs who will turn a trick when they 'feel like it ' or need the money and who are either ignorant of the rules of conduct or cannot be bothered to stick to them. They lack the abilities and skills needed to make a living out of prostitution. These amateurs are the ones who determine the image of male prostitution, even to the extent that nowadays they are looked upon as the core of male prostitution by nearly every expert all over the world.

Of course there are organized forms of male prostitution that accompany the street cultures. Prostitutes in this sector differ from street prostitutes in that they do not stand alone. Some activities are taken out of their hands by the madam, who attracts the customers, provides the 'relaxing rooms' and guarantees the safety of both the prostitutes and customers. These facilities are open to the male prostitutes who are willing to give up their independence by entering the service of the madam. In exchange for a percentage of their earnings they are licensed to exploit the company formula in the name of the madam. In this sector a bourgeois atmosphere is predominant. A relatively large number of the customers are tourists, but there are also locals, who consider their visit an outing. They take their time and appreciate conversations that surpass the sexual character of their meeting. It is difficult for male prostitutes who lack in verbal skills or sufficient knowledge of foreign languages to hold their ground in this sector, unless they have entered the service of one of the Amsterdam clubs where the management is in charge of the whole process and leaves the boys only limited scope to act independently. In this club they are directed to act according to a formula that aims at selling as much champagne as possible. In this organized sector the most professional prostitutes are experts at finding affluent customers whom they charm by acting as the type of guy the customer fancies.

Other groups also exist, for example 'call boys'. In this sector male prostitutes offer their services through ads in newspapers and gay magazines. They operate independently and date men over the telephone. The prostitutes either receive them at home, or visit them in hotels or in the homes of their customers. Their clients are mainly ultra-secretive homosexuals who are afraid of having their tendencies known.

'Top hats' are the last group to mention here, these are the innovatory businessmen. They have outgrown the regular prostitution premises and individually found new outlets. They cater for the needs of men who preferably abstain from employing the services of male prostitutes, but would like to be seen in the company of a young, newly captured companion, and who are willing to pay for it.

Seen from a professional point of view, as Van der Poel argues, male prostitution is a commercial service-oriented occupation with economic and social characteristics that are typical of other branches of small and medium sized businesses. As independent entrepreneurs, prostitutes have to move with the times and adapt to the demands of the market. That is where the key to success in this profession is to be found, he argues.

Boys in Prostitution (primarily from Zuilhof, 1995)

Boys working in prostitution are considered an HIV risk group in the Netherlands. They are considered as such, as part of the risk group of 'men with homosexual contacts', which remains the largest risk group, because of the estimated number of their partners, and their material dependence on these partners. A substantial proportion of the boys are considered to be at even greater risk, because of intravenous drug use.

Little is known about the spread of the virus among boy-prostitutes. No specific epidemiological research has been carried out. A recent behaviouristic study among a small number of Dutch boys indicated that there are two types of prostitutes who are probably taking a larger risk. The first group consists of boys who identify themselves with being homosexual, and permit themselves to have sexual feelings during commercial contacts, especially when they are working in settings where sexual contacts can take place in a quiet, personal and intimate atmosphere, and in cases where receptive anal contact is in their repertoire. The second group consists of heavy drug addicts, who sometimes have to work when their need for a drug becomes acute. They are less choosy in their selection of clients, and when in need they take any risk.

The above mentioned results of the study are making it clear that boys working in prostitution cannot be approached as a uniform group. There is great diversity among them. This diversity is manifested not only by the boys' various sexual identifications, whether they use drugs and to what extent they do, but also by their diverse types of prostitution, and the number of the boys' nationalities as well. During the last few years at least twenty nationalities, together with fourteen mother languages were represented in Amsterdam.

Street Prostitution

There is also a large diversity in lifestyles. The boys who work in the streets are mostly homeless boys who use intravenous drugs. But this cannot be considered characteristic for all of them. In Amsterdam, and, for instance, in Berlin, there are many Romanian boys working in the streets who do not use intravenous drugs. In Amsterdam, these are predominantly individually operating present or past asylum seekers, who either live in refugee camps waiting for the results of their asylum application, or are homeless. In Berlin, the Romanian boys are often younger, at 14–16 years, and they live with their families. There are also Turkish and Moroccan boys (some of them illegally living in the Netherlands), working in Amsterdam, and who are not homeless either. Hardly any of the Moroccan, Turkish or Romanian boys consider themselves homosexual, although insertive anal contact is often accepted by Turkish and Moroccan boys; Romanian boys sometimes have problems with it.

A considerable proportion of Dutch boys working in the streets consider themselves homosexual or bisexual. Many of them use drugs, but most of them not intravenously, and under some control. Some of them are homeless. Many German boys working in the streets have come to Amsterdam as intravenous addicts, and these are often homeless.

In the clubs of Amsterdam, the diversity in nationalities is probably even greater. On the other hand, a certain group behaviour seems to occur, which reduces the diversity in lifestyles. The group behaviour is manifested by mutual sexual relationships and collective visits to discos. These boys predominantly do not take intravenous drugs, but many of them do take hashish and weed and some of them take ecstasy and cocaine.

Czech boys can often be distinguished from other boys in the Amsterdam clubs by their behaviour. They are present in the clubs at different times and to different extents. They are the only nationality who do not come on their own initiative but are organised by others and taken to Amsterdam. Most of them only speak Czech. In contrast to most other boys in the clubs they call themselves heterosexuals, are mostly living in the clubs where they work, and have a different living pattern, which sometimes includes prostitution. So, the diversity in a city like Amsterdam is enormous, and the descriptions above do not include prostitutes working as escorts, or at home!

Behavioural Aspects

A substantial step towards a greater insight into the situation is getting to know the most important personal motivations: 'Why did a particular boy decide to start working in prostitution?' The answer 'In order to earn money' is not always correct. A great number of boys did not make this decision for financial reasons. Their highest priority was to get some attention and safety or to satisfy their sexual needs. For some of the boys, stepping into prostitution implied a positive step in developing their own homosexual identity. An answer to not only this question but also the knowledge of the boys' motivation to go on supplies the information needed for effective AIDS prevention. Such knowledge provides an insight into the behavioural motives that determine whether the boys take risks regarding HIV or not.

In reality, the 'materialistic' and 'psychological' motivations are probably connected, but one of the two, the one that has higher priority at that moment, often determines whether the boy takes risks or not. As proven in the above mentioned study among Dutch boys, boys who are dope addicts will, at times when they feel a great need for using a drug, certainly give a higher priority to earning the money they need for the drug than to safe sex. At the same time, there are boys who report never having had unsafe sex just for money; sometimes they possibly might do it, but only when they are in love.

The second group of boys described in the study who take risks illustrates that many boys experience commercial sex as very close to their own experience of lust. If these contacts are their only opportunity to have sex with male partners (a psychological motivation), safe sex can definitely not be guaranteed. For the boys who make a clear distinction between commercial and private sex, the latter plays a significant role. These are the contacts they have with each other, or with partners whom they meet by going out. These boys often make a clear distinction between on the one hand, having sex with clients, and on the other hand, with persons they feel lust for.

In the latter case, they have a different attitude towards the risk of HIV: the risk is denied, ignored or not experienced which leads to unsafe sex with these partners.

Interventions

These various aspects make it clear that good AIDS prevention, targeted at boys working in prostitution, should go further than providing knowledge on the risks of HIV and supplying condoms. If we miss out on their motivations, we can never influence the determinants of their behaviour. This means that an effective HIV prevention programme cannot be approached, apart from assistance in other spheres. For instance, many homeless boys who are drug-addicts, will only give safe sex a higher priority, if they are provided with shelter and good social assistance regarding drugs and, consequently, if they are able to take a more independent stance, with respect to the clients and their wishes. Boys, whose contacts with their desired partners depend on men who pay for them, should get a practical and psychological opportunity to seek partners, in a setting where equality and free choice are permitted. A possible alternative is a 'coming out', leading to a stronger homosexual identity.

For many of the above-mentioned types of boys, prostitution is a nega-tive choice. The task of social assistance should be to aim at making the un-real alternative of 'coming out' more possible. An effective HIV prevention programme should not be limited to conveying information. Regarding the above described determinants, interventions at the level of personal attitudes and behavioural skills are necessary as well.

In the message conveyed in these interventions, their work as prostitutes must be approached in a positive way: the problem is HIV, not prostitution. Safe sex must be linked to professionality in their work. In contrast to what is often being claimed, information about the risks of HIV can be supplied better by a professional in health care, for instance a doctor, than by a peer educator. A lot of the boys are anxious about possible risks; they have difficult questions and are very critical. A peer educator is, in many cases, not able to do away with the anxiety. The information should be supplied repeatedly, as the boys often begin to have doubts after hearing other, perhaps incorrect stories. Good leaflets, in various languages, may be of great support. These leaflets must be small, so that they can be easily hidden in a pocket, and specifically targeted at the boys.

Interventions at the levels of attitude and behavioural skills, may be made more effective by a source who is closer to them, like a familiar and trusted professional educator, or social worker, or, what is often even better, a source 'from inside' (a peer). This often implies 'empowerment': for some of them empowerment as professional sex workers, for others as boys with a homosexual identity, or as reasonable drug-users, or as HIV positive sex workers. Educators and social workers can stimulate this process of empowerment, for instance, through organising meetings with boys in more or less similar situations. In this way, for example in a meeting of boys using drugs, the boys can learn from each other, since all of them are in the same situation, how better to combine paid sex and dope, and avoiding the risk of HIV.

General Descriptions

Girls

The following description would typify a group of young female prostitutes in a Dutch city. The composition of the group is rather heterogeneous as to the girls' backgrounds and ages. There are girls of Dutch origin as well as girls with Surinamese, Turkish, Hindustani and Italian backgrounds. The proportions are, respectively, approximately 60 per cent Dutch and 40 per cent the other nationalities. Most of the girls still live with their parents; a few of them live on their own (or cohabit with their boyfriend). A few of them live in boarding-schools. Most of them still attend school and a few of them have a job on the side in supermarkets on Saturdays. The girls truant regularly. Most of them who do not go to school any more have jobs, all of these jobs have been created in line with a special arrangement (so called 'experience-gaining jobs'). What all of them have in common is a poor education and few social contacts outside their jobs and schools. The reason why they can meet is the aerobics training in the community youth centre on Monday evenings. Moreover, the centre is closed to boys on Mondays!

These two aspects give the girls a legitimate opportunity to leave their homes, with the permission of their parents, educators or partners. After the training, the girls are used to spending quite a long time drinking tea and chatting a lot. The subjects vary widely, such as school, home situation, job, appearance, and above all, sexuality. Instead of the aerobic training, a lecture or discussion on a particular topic by professional physicians, cosmeticians, dieticians etc. is organised from time to time.

Street prostitution

The 'typical' group described here is of boys in a city, working in street prostitution. Many of them come from socially weak families and have received little affection in their homes. A considerable proportion of the boys are drug-addicts: homo-prostitution is their source of incomes with which they can buy heroin and cocaine. The prostitutes can be divided into two sub-groups: a group of relatively good-looking new boys, and a group of boys who have been doing the job for a longer time and whom one can immediately spot as drug-users. In street prostitution, the prices are lower than in brothels, and there is strong competition, especially between the various nationalities: they accuse each other of having prices that are too low. Despite the competition, friendships between the boys, and sometimes even more intimate contacts occur. Some of the boys say that they would like to leave this way of life but only a few of them actually do so. It is partly connected with the fact that, in a short time and easily, they earn a relatively large amount of money. Moreover, most of the boys have almost nothing else but this way of life. If they get out of it, they have nothing else.

Boarding houses

The target group is composed of youngsters, aged 12 to 18 living in a boarding-house. The group can be described as a group of problem youths, a considerable proportion of whom have criminal backgrounds. There are several different groups within the boarding-house. Youngsters from the ages 12 to 14 are divided into a special group for boys and a special group for girls; the groups of the 'older' ones from 14 to 18 are mixed. The boarding-house is situated out of the way and forms a very closed community. Because of its closed nature, the young people know almost everything about each other. Most of them stay here approximately one year. The young people attend a boarding school. A limited group of them is allowed to leave the community and go home at the weekends.

Prevention (primarily from Reinders, 1995)

Worldwide, sexual intercourse proves to be the main transmission route for HIV, followed by the routes of intravenous drug use (IDU) and of vertical transmission from mother to child. Finally, HIV infections are contracted through blood and blood products. Only in Europe has the transmission through blood and blood products been effectively blocked. The prevention activities undertaken so far have contributed to the stabilisation and even decrease of the HIV infection rate in homosexual men. These activities have to be continued, focusing on young homo- and bisexual men and on the behaviour maintenance of older men. Additionally, extra attention is also needed for the prevention of HIV infections among heterosexuals and intravenous drug-users, where unprotected sexual intercourse and needle sharing present the highest elements of risk. AIDS education programmes must be aimed at modifying sexual and drug use risk behaviours. Besides its fatality, the epidemic also causes unease and distrust. Moreover, there is a prevailing discrimination against HIV positive people, people with AIDS and members of groups in which a higher rate of infection exists, such as homosexuals and drug-users, and this discrimination may even result in or increase homophobia. Another goal of AIDS education programmes therefore is the prevention of unnecessary fear, distrust and discrimination.

Interventions: Education and Empowerment

Because of the increase in the number of homeless young people, refugees and infected girls and women, more and more broad interventions are required. These must be interventions which focus not only on education but also on a supporting and health promoting environment. Therefore, a close collaboration of the public and private sector is required. Excluded youth like the homeless, marginalised youth and children in difficult circumstances, youth who are outside the social system and who lack access to services and information, do not only need education but also empowerment through their environment. Their vulnerability is especially increased since they are often exposed to adult exploitation including incest, sexual abuse and violence and the sex trade. Their risk behaviour, their lack of self-esteem, food, money, education and intimacy, and their bad physical and emotional conditions require not only education and prevention but, in an integrated way, also care. Prevention programmes must be expanded in a way that mobilises society as a whole. An important, adequate strategy could be the development of regional and local networks between health care, youth workers, teachers, pupil guides and the youth themselves.

Strategies

The following model has been described by Kok and De Vries, (1989). Planned health education is a form of planned behavioural change, consisting of two phases, planning, and an evaluation.

Figure 1: Planning			
Health Problem	Related Behaviour	Intervention Determinants	Implementation Strategy

In the planning phase an attempt to answer five questions is made:
1. How serious is the problem?
2. Which behaviour is involved?
3. What are the determinants of that behaviour?
4. What options are there for change (intervention)?
5. How can these options be implemented?

The first two steps, analysing the problem, (AIDS), and analysing the behaviour, such as unsafe sex and needle sharing, are often most efficiently dealt with by epidemiologists. The task for health promoters is to carefully plan and evaluate the interventions.

Determinants of Behaviour

Health education starts with a clear behavioural goal. We have both an undesired and desired, that is, preventive behaviour, and we want people to change from behaving in the undesired way. Once we have a clear behavioural goal, we try to change the behaviour determinants, be it attitude, social influence or efficacy and barriers. Changing by health education means changing by communication. Therefore the first goal is to get attention for the message. The second goal is to change the determinants of behaviour. The third and last goal is the maintenance of the behavioural change. A one time only change is not enough. We want the desired behaviour to become a habit. For an answer to the question of behaviour determinants we lean upon social-psychological theories and models. There are three kinds of determinants:

- attitude
- social influence
- efficacy/barriers

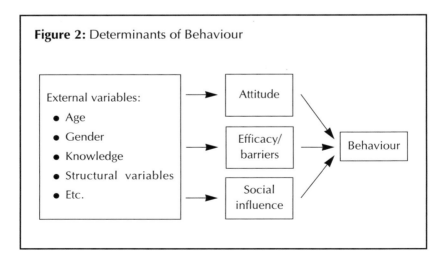

Figure 2: Determinants of Behaviour

Attitude

An attitude to behaviour is the weighing of all the advantages and disadvantages of performing that behaviour. Health is only one of the possible considerations, and is often a relatively unimportant one among youth and especially among excluded youth. When health is considered to be part of the attitude, we can suppose that the motivation to act in a manner conductive to good health is a combination of the perceived severity of the health risk and the effectiveness of the preventive behaviour. But, again, health considerations are mostly not dominant and other considerations such as costs, likes and dislikes, and status are more important. Knowledge about health risks alone generally proves not to be related to behavioural change.

Social influences (social norm)

This refers to the influence of others, either directly, through what others expect, or indirectly, through what others do (modelling). Social influence is often underestimated as a determinant of behaviour. Social-psychological studies show that social influence can lead to behaviour that conflicts with one's own previous attitudes. The bases for social influences have two principles. Firstly, people like to have the right information, and the ideas and behaviour of other people are sources of information. Secondly, people like to receive social rewards, such as getting compliments from others and belonging to a group. People are often quite unaware themselves of the strong influence others have on their own behaviour.

For example, parents and peers form an important source of information and influence with respect to sexuality. Most studies suggest that the ideas of the partner, peers and parents about AIDS prevention and condom use either influence the attitude to condom use, or directly influence the use of condoms. Based on this we can conclude that in AIDS education it is very useful to pay attention to the development of positive group norms with respect to condom use. It is also important to insure this group against a possible resistance of peers towards condom use. Support from their environment strongly influences the realisation of behavioural changes.

Efficacy/barriers

Is the person equipped to perform the desired behaviour? Self-efficacy is an estimation of the ability to cope with possible barriers inside or outside the person. Examples of the former might be not enough knowledge, or not enough abilities. Examples of outside barriers could be resistance from others, or not enough support and access to provisions, time and money not available, and perhaps conflicting life styles.

Self-efficacy is the perception of the ability to perform the behaviour, whilst barriers are the real problems people face, sometimes unexpectedly, in actually behaving. Self-efficacy is shaped by experiences with barriers, experiences with successes, vicarious learning, verbal persuasion and physiological information.

There is a logical relation between perceived efficacy and real barriers, but there is also an important relation between efficacy and success in performing the behaviour. People with a higher efficacy naturally have a higher chance of succeeding, independent of real barriers. But the discrepancy between perceived efficacy and real barriers should not become too large. Health promoters can try to increase perceived self-efficacy in order to motivate people to perform the preventive behaviour. At the same time, they should help people to overcome the real barriers to performing that behaviour.

Other possible factors, say, external variables, are supposed to influence behaviour through these three main determinants. If there is a relationship between sex and behaviour, there will be a difference between boys and girls with respect to attitude, social influence and the efficacy/barriers affecting that behaviour.

Take, for example, that communicative skills are very important to condom use because of AIDS. The more trust people have in their own skills with respect to talking and negotiating about condom use, the more they may be willing to use condoms. It is thus very important to actually practice buying condoms and to practice the skills necessary to use the condom.

The Goals of AIDS Education

Alongside the prevention of discrimination, various specific goals of AIDS education programmes for preventing HIV infection include abstinence of sexual contacts, postponing sexual intercourse, reducing the number of partners, practising safe sex, no intravenous drug-use or only practising safe drug use through using sterile needles. Aware that mere knowledge is not enough to change behaviour, the following subsidiary aims, which delineate three elements necessary for behavioural change, have to be achieved:

Knowledge of	Attitude towards	Skills in
sexuality, drug use and AIDS	being aware of one's own values and behaviour/habits	saying 'no'
sexual and drug use attitudes and behaviours of others	having a realistic risk perception	communicating about safer sex/ safe drug use
own risk and non-risk behaviour	being convinced of the effectiveness of one's own coping skills (self-efficacy)	negotiating about safer sex/safe drug use
preventative measures		buying and using condoms
the impact of AIDS on individuals and society	having a positive attitude towards safe sex, negotiating alternatives to penetrative sex and the use of sterile needles	obtaining and using sterile needles
health services for young people		using health services and relevant provisions adequately
	being confident that condoms protect against STDs and AIDS	
	being convinced that in using i.v. drugs only sterile needles protect against the HIV virus	
	being convinced that HIV infected people need love and care instead of isolation	
	being convinced that everyone has a right of access to health services	

A complete AIDS prevention programme should focus on one or more of these goals. This implies that programmes should not only offer correct knowledge but also promote attitudes and training skills through methods. Information on what people think of specific issues is important in designing health promotion strategies, messages, and materials. For planning AIDS health promotion, information is needed rapidly. Rapid assessment techniques, usually involving the use of small surveys, group interviews, and in-depth individual interviews with members of key target groups and community workers, can provide the preliminary information needed for health promotion, (*Guide*, WHO, 1989). Some information will be available from earlier studies and reports; some information will have to be collected by the planning team. However, the gathering of information for health promotion planning should not be allowed to significantly delay the health promotion action.

Messages

A health promotion strategy is a planned approach for the achievement of a health promotion objective. The planning and development of programme strategies should be based on the initial assessment as well as on information about the target group as it becomes available. The development of health promotion programme strategies is a continually dynamic process, (*Guide*, WHO, 1989). Strategy development includes the development of messages and materials and the selection of appropriate channels of communication, institutional networks, and activities for reaching target groups with the messages. It also deals with the way to combine different messages and channels so that they reinforce and complement each other.

Ideological or Realistic Messages: Some Concluding Thoughts

Knowing the data of the sexual behaviour of youth and the effects of mass media openness on sexuality, it is an important question whether the restriction of the safe sex message in 'no sex' or 'abstinence of sex' is still attractive, persuading and reliable enough to effectively reach youth. Between 'no sex' and 'safe sex' there is a dilemma for a lot of health educators. Should we guide young people towards a healthy self-esteem and sexual growth and development, respecting the right to sexuality and to their own choices of 'no sex', 'safer sex' or 'safe sex'? Or should we, in the perspectives of religious and cultural views, strive to discourage youth from having any sexual activity and deny the existence of this element of human beings in their growth and development.

In order to be able to control the epidemic of AIDS, we can never close our eyes to the current sexual behaviour of youth.

The tensions between some of these differences are too great to simply 'square'. However, harm reductionist based health interventionist strategies and practices are being developed and applied in the Netherlands against a backdrop of a predominantly international supply and demand element of their economy—that of their youth sex industry.

References

Barrett, D. (1994). Social Policies on the Street: Responding to Juvenile Prostitutes in Amsterdam, London and Paris. *Social Work in Europe*, Vol. 1; No 1: pp 29–32.

WHO (1989). *Guide to Planning Health Promotion for AIDS Prevention Control*. Geneva: WHO AIDS Series 5.

Kok, G. and Vries, H. de (1989). *Primary Prevention of Cancers: The Need for Health Education and Intersectoral Health Promotion in Reducing the Risks of Cancers*. England: Open University Press.

O'Neill, M. (1991). *Routes into Prostitution: Poverty, Homelessness and Leaving Care*. Paper available from the author at University of Staffordshire, England.

Reinders, J. (1995). Planning Health Promotion for AIDS Prevention and Control. In Reiners, J. and Vermeer, V. (Eds.). *How to Reach Youth Outside the School Setting*. Woerden: Dutch Centre for Health Promotion and Health Education.

Stichting Streetcornerwork (1999). Jaarverslang 1998, Werkplan 1999/2000 from *Streetcornerwork*. Amsterdam, Juli 1999.

Van der Ploeg, J. (1989). Homelessness: A Multi-dimensional Problem. *Children and Youth Services Review*, Vol. 11: pp 45–56.

Van der Poel, S. (1991). *In de Bisnis: Professionele Jongensprostitute in Amsterdam*. Arnhem: Gouda Quint BV.

Vena Newsletter (1989). Editorial comment, Vol. 1; No. 2: p 1.

Zuilhof, W. (1995). Boys in Prostitution and Prevention on AIDS. In Reiners, J. and Vermeer, V. (Eds.). *How to Reach Youth Outside the School Setting*. Woerden: Dutch Centre for Health Promotion and Health Education.

Chapter 7

Youth Prostitution in Romania

Doina Nistor and Contiu Tiberiu Cristi Soitu

Introduction

Romania lies in South Eastern Europe, with an area of 91,600 square miles and a population of 22.5 million. The Latin origin of the people and the Christian Orthodox religion of the majority represent a unique combination. Ten years ago we saw the fall of communism in Europe, and thus the political system changed almost simultaneously with other Eastern European countries. The difficulties in Romania and the economic, social and political tensions that followed in the 'transition' process had repercussions on the system of values. Based on this background, the increase in crime has become quasi-general, without considering what is acceptable as a 'normal' value.

Like everywhere in the world, prostitution has been a constant presence in Romanian society. The two major turning points for prostitution during this century have been the integration of prostitutes into socialist society in the 1940s and its increasing visibility in current years. This chapter considers the causes of Romanian prostitution, many of which are tied in some way to economic factors, and it looks briefly at past and current legislation and discusses the typology of both prostitutes and procurers. Statistical data in the pre-Revolution era are lacking, but recent data are provided in order that age, educational status and the background of 'perpetrators' can be considered. The current situation, particularly involving prostitution among young people is unsatisfactory. A fundamental change in outlook is required.

The Causes of Prostitution in Romania

In Romania, the causes of prostitution are determined directly by the economic context. Unemployment is one of the major factors, if we take into account the process of economic reform that resulted in the loss of numerous jobs.

This is more prominent in the case of young women, with little or no seniority. A low level of income and difficult work conditions turn young women with material problems to either occasional prostitution or to prostitution on a more consistent basis. Women from families within a deficient educational climate, often dysfunctional, lacking paternal authority, alcoholism, truancy and school dropouts, are open to the negative influence of their social environment. Others are introduced to the business by procurers, and sometimes they can be relatives of the women, or by 'recruiters'.

But in Romania, as in other countries, prostitution is determined not only by the economic context, but also by other factors:

- Personal family failure: many prostitutes are divorced women, often with a child to care for.
- Engaging in sexual relations at an early age: in some cases, before 15 years old.
- Previous sexual assault suffered at a young age.
- 'Occupational affinity' which is an involvement in a profession practised in similar contexts to those of prostitution i.e. waitresses, cocktail waitresses, sales assistants, or entertainers. Sometimes, the owners abused them, or the occasions for prostitution appeared frequently.
- The attraction of prostitution, perceived as an interesting profession, with little routine, with lack of difficulties and with tempting perspectives.

According to police reports, after 1990, the phenomenon of prostitution and procuring has seen changes consistent with the evolution of the socio-economic situation in Romania. There are two known reasons for the manifestation of the phenomenon. Firstly, some of the prostitutes, active in 1990, who had some assets in lei or in hard currency went into association with procurers and set up commercial businesses as a cover and continued actively recruiting and placing girls. Secondly, workers who spent a short period working abroad, returned to Romania to recruit young women for various jobs, such as dancers, cocktail waitresses, chambermaids. Upon their arrival in the country of destination, these women would be forced into prostitution.

Romanian Legislation

The legislative evolution began to develop around the beginning of the 19th century, (1812), in Iasi—the ancient capital of the Moldavian Principality, the eastern part of Romania—a restricted and controlled area, ('La Madammes'), in which brothels were permitted. In 1933, the Romanian Parliament stipulated very clearly by law that the prostitutes were obliged to undergo regular medical check-ups. This 'profession' was officially eradicated after the Second World War. For example (Article 328: The Romanian Criminal Code, title IX (Offences that hurt certain relations concerning social cohabitation), chapter IV (Other offences that hurt certain relations concerning social cohabitation)):

> *Prostitution—the act of the person who earns one's living or whose principal livelihood is achieved by sexual intercourse with various individuals shall be punished by imprisonment from three months to three years.*

By criminalising prostitution, the legislator intended to assure the respect of the norms by which each individual has to procure one's livelihood through honest work; also in mind was the defence of moral values concerning the sexual and public life of the individuals.

For the offence of prostitution to be considered, the law requires the existence of sexual intercourse with several separate partners and not with one individual only. If the sexual intercourse involves only one partner, and thus the requirements of the law are not met, the act does not constitute an offence of prostitution. It is considered an immoral act but not an illegal one.

Another example is Article 329:

> *Whoremongering (procuring)—urging or forcing into prostitution, facilitating the practice of prostitution, gaining profit as a result of somebody's prostitution activity, and also one's conscription to practice prostitution or the traffic of persons with this purpose is punished with imprisonment from two to seven years and the banning of certain civil rights.*

If these offences are committed upon a child or presents other aggravating characteristics, the punishment consists of imprisonment from three to ten years and the banning of certain civil rights.

> *Money, values or any other goods which have served or have been destined to serve directly or indirectly in committing the offence described in the paragraphs 1 and 2, as well as those obtained by committing it, are confiscated; if they are not found, the offender has to pay their equivalent in money.*

The attempt to commit this act is also punished (as it was changed by Law No. 140/1996).

This article of law, (328), has been modified twice, once in 1993, when punishments were increased, and again in 1996 when punishments were reduced. At the moment the general tendency is to legalise prostitution and there already exists a law project concerned with setting up private brothels under the state's control. Two members of the Romanian Parliament, Ioan-Adrian Vilau and Mariana Stoica have had an initiative in this respect. The intention to legalise this phenomenon is motivated by the greater possibility of medical, social and law enforcement with economical control. Because the legal system is at once an embodiment of morality and a means by which we deal with conflicts and problems, (Hart, 1961), laws must reflect a wide spectrum of people's needs if they are to be effective.

Opponents of the current laws emphasise that they are:

- Unfair: they embody one set of moral beliefs—those of social conservatives, vice squad personnel, the Moral Majority, and misogynists —and ignore other, equally important interests—women, children, liberals, and feminists.

- Ineffective: they criminalise prostitution, thereby contributing to the current legal morass in the criminal justice system in which petty crimes pre-empt court time and drain the system of resources.

- Costly: in penalising prostitution, it costs local and central (national) governments a lot of money yearly by contributing to the expense of maintaining the 'revolving door' through which the arrested—in the most central places—are merely recycled through the system and are back out onto the street within hours.

- Counterproductive: prostitution cannot be eradicated but only controlled. Because criminalisation ostracises prostitution, there is little likelihood of rehabilitation.

Most critics stress that decriminalisation, which entails a hands-off policy, offers the only viable option, although they concede that many local citizens would be incensed at police-protected areas of vice. Under this policy, police would no longer be able to detain prostitutes, use them as informants, or arrest them simply to enhance their arrest quotas. Prostitutes would receive the same protection under the law as any other citizen and would no longer be prime targets for violent crime. Decriminalisation would restore independence for most prostitutes and insure greater street safety. A more humane policy would also emancipate prostitution from the criminal underworld and offer greater opportunities for prostitutes to seek conventional friends and social services.

A Typology of Romanian Prostitutes

The world of prostitution is a special sub-culture that has its own values, hierarchies, and members. It consists of prostitutes, pimps, ushers, leaders, the lesbian prostitutes' lovers and matrons, and also includes security agents and policemen.

Prostitution is shaped by its sex-for-profit basis; its illegal status raises costs, encourages police corruption, and increases the likelihood of crime, such as theft and mutual assault. Prostitution increases in times of high unemployment or high inflation, as is the current situation in Romania. Low wages serve as an inducement to involving women in the sex trades, i.e. working as models for sex magazines or films or as live performers in the proliferating pornography industry, from which many drift into full-time prostitution.

Recent analyses of cases, and research concerning the impact of the Romanian society democratisation on human behaviour, developing the problems of some specific deviant forms, identifies the phenomenon of prostitution as one of the most frequent and more visible in public opinion (see G.M. Botescu, PhD thesis). The same conclusions were obtained also by the 'Trinational Group' which held an open seminar in Iasi, Romania (May–June, 1998)— Prostitution among Children and Adolescents.

Concerning prostitutes 'class', the author found a kind of 'specialisation' as follows:

Street Walkers: These represent the most common and visible type of prostitutes who 'work' in the crowded areas of the cities. They are the ones most exposed to police, violent clients and to the abuse of pimps. These women work on a delineated area, and between them there are those protected by pimps (he protects his 'girls' from violent clients in various ways: i.e. threats and retaining an identity document) and those who refuse the pimps' protection. Streetwalkers come from marginal areas, from disadvantaged categories of people and they are involved also in other illegal activities: robberies, abetting of thieves, and drug trafficking. A lot of them are introduced to the 'profession' by other prostitutes or by pimps.

B-Girls: This category is on a higher level in the hierarchy. The women work undercover integrating with the usual clientele in bars, restaurants, hotels, and discos. The B-Girls work habitually in collaboration with the owner of the business, who protects them from police raids. These 'girls' are called or contacted by previously selected customers.

Brothel Prostitutes: The most common type of prostitution in Romania during the period between the two World Wars. The main towns had their own red light districts i.e. The Stone Cross ('Crucea de Piatra') in Bucharest, 'At

Madame's' ('La Madame') in Iasi. At present, the brothels are clandestine and they are owned by procurers who sequester the girls in order to give the girls more clients in exchange for less money or for no money at all.

Masseuse Prostitutes: There are some so-called 'massage parlours' in Bucharest, but although there is not enough official information about their activity, one regards them as acting as a front for prostitution.

Strip Girl Prostitutes: They do not have sexual intercourse with the customers, but they offer an 'artistic service' behind a window. This kind of prostitution is not frequent in Romania, and is seen more in the bigger cities.

Call Girls: This is the 'aristocracy' of prostitution. They work without pimps, their clients are from high society and their prices are exhorbitant (starting at 1,000 dollars a day). Usually, their academic level is very high.

Escort Girls: This is a specialisation where the demand exceeds the supply in an expanding 'market'.

Circumstantial Prostitution: This is practised usually by middle-aged divorced women who have either no job or a cash flow problem.

Male Prostitution: A difference must be made between homosexual and heterosexual prostitution, the former being the most common. There are several types of homosexual prostitution: full-time professionals, part-time hustlers, kept boys and several types of heterosexual male prostitution, gigolos and private secretaries etc.

Child Prostitution

This is a phenomenon which applies particularly to children from disorganised and disadvantaged families and the majority of them are street children. According to the European Council's definition, it involves 'children or adolescents under 18 years of age who live on the streets for long or short periods, move from one place to another, have their own group of friends and contacts; also children living at home with parents or in state-run institutions'. They have little or no contact with adults or with these institutions.

After 1990, these children became a visible reality in Romania, a reality that accompanies the critical social events in the present period of transition. The analyses made on this aspect and the projects designed to reduce this phenomenon, gave emphasis to some specific characteristics. Firstly, this phenomenon cannot be denied; it is in evolution but it is proportionally less than in other Eastern European countries. It is evident in several big cities, especially Bucharest, although some of the children come from other towns or cities. A great number of the children involved have run away from families, orphanages or childcare institutions. The majority of them come from families that have problems in their social and professional integration. Also included are children who alternate living at home (with their families or in childcare institutions) and living on the streets; almost all of them could be (potentially) re-integrated into society.

In Bucharest, for example, there are an estimated 1,500 street children, but this number doesn't include the children who 'work' all day long, that is, those who beg and return home in the evening. It must be noted that the percentage of girls is lower than that of boys: there are only 17.5 per cent girls in this category. The majority of these children are aged between 12 and 16, the average age being 14. The average age of the girls is only 13. It has been noted that the groups of street children tend to be homogenous depending on age.

Most of these children, over 60 per cent of them, come from dysfunctional families: 36.2 per cent have parents who have separated, 15 per cent have deceased parents, 5 per cent have an arrested parent and a further 5 per cent are abandoned children. Some children have left childcare institutions in search of a life of adventure or simple curiosity. For the majority of these children, poverty was not the main issue for leaving home, family or care institution, originally, and they prefer living on the streets.

The highest density of homeless children in Romania is in Bucharest, by the North Railway Station area. There are several reasons for this:

- Children from the provinces who have left home congregate there.
- It is a commercial area and is considered an area where money can be 'earned' more easily through more or less legal activities.
- The railway station and its neighbourhood, with trains, waiting rooms, sewers and so on, offer opportunities for accommodation. The great ebb and flow of people travelling and also the vicinity of the parking areas— where the foreign coaches and cars are parked—helped to establish prostitution and procuring.

The need to survive and to fulfil childhood desires, for sweets, cakes etc., make these children easy victims. In many of the cases in which they are involved their 'reward' consists only in security—for a short time.

A Typology of Procurers

The procurers are the intermediaries between the prostitutes and customers, protecting them from interference with the law and clients. They try to ensure the girls avoid arrest, perhaps by asserting that they are their girlfriends or trying to bribe the police; they pay lawyers and bails; if both of them, procurer and girl, are arrested, the girl has priority in getting free again; they take care of the prostitutes' children during their mother's arrest; they protect the girls against violent clients and they pay for medical treatment when the prostitutes need it. Until 1990, a large number of the prostitutes' clients were gypsies but after 1990 some of them became procurers. As in the case of prostitutes, there is also a typology of procurers:

Street Procurers: Each procurer has 3–5 girls whom he directs on a well-delineated area, having access to a hotel or an apartment. The concept of 'personal managers' is also used.

Procurers—Brothel Owners: They are the most dangerous as the brothels resemble prisons, the girls are totally deprived of their freedom and the brothel owners have the financial benefit from the girls' activities. The girls receive no financial gain and are expected to have sexual intercourse with up to 20 customers a day; a lack of performance could result in murder.

Procurers—Bar (Disco) Owners: This is a category of procurers originating from former street procurers who bought a bar or a disco with money earned during their past business.

Matrons (The Madams): There are two types in this category: firstly, modern matrons, young former prostitutes who consider this kind of activity as easier and more lucrative, and secondly, classical matrons, old women who were not previously professional prostitutes.

'Swagwomen': These women rent their rooms by the hour to prostitutes without any other involvement. They see themselves as 'honest women'.

Panders or Ushers: They find clients for the prostitutes, for a smaller commission fee than the procurers.

Statistical Data Concerning the Evolution of Juvenile Prostitution in Romania in the Context of the General Phenomenon

Romanian statistics regarding prostitution are incomplete and often contain inaccurate data, and do not reflect its evolution in its entirety in the period either before or after 1989, although prostitution had been practised in various organised or unorganised forms, covert or overt, in the previous decades. In general, there are no officially published data concerning prostitution in the communist period, although these data were known by the working authorities involved.

After 1989 the first statistical records concerning prostitution began being discretely recorded by the police. From the data provided by the General Inspectorate of Police, the following outlines this phenomenon in the period after the Revolution.

Table 1: The Evolution of the Phenomenon of Prostitution

Year	Number of crimes	Crimes proportion: current year/total	Increase
1990	10	0.38 per cent	–
1991	112	4.3 per cent	1020 per cent
1995	698	26 per cent	523 per cent
1996	730	28 per cent	4 per cent
1997	1039	40 per cent	42 per cent
Total	2589	100 per cent	–

As it can be seen, although the data is incomplete, there is a progressive evolution, with most of the infractions being committed in 1997. The data available shows a fairly spectacular increase in the first years, and one could assume that the phenomenon could have been greater but its real extent is unknown.

Table 2: Statistical Data Concerning the Proportion of Infractions/Authors and Pimping (Procuring)/ Prostitution

		Children	%	Adults	%	Girls/ women	%	Boys/ men	%
No. of crimes	**Prostitution**	185	30	425	70				
	Procuring	59	13	370	87				
Total		244	23	795	77				
No. of offenders	**Prostitution**	137	22	479	78	607	98	9	2
	Procuring	17	4	397	96	139	33	275	67
Total		154		873		746		284	

In 1997, it is noticeable that the ratio of pimping (procuring) infractions to prostitution infractions is 70:30 and the ratio pimps to prostitutes is 66:33. The proportion of under age persons involved in prostitution is 30 per cent of the total. Women represent 98 per cent, men 2 per cent of the total. The women involved in procuring represent 33 per cent of the total.

Table 3: Statistical Data Concerning Prostitution Depending in Relation to the Age of the Perpetrators

Age	Procurers (Pc)		Prostitutes (Ps)		Proportions	
	No.	%	No.	%	Pc %	Ps %
−13	0	0	1	0	0	0
14–18	19	4.5	157	25.5	10.7	89.3
19–20	45	11	163	26.5	21.6	78.3
21–30	178	43	256	41.5	41	59
31–50	149	36	38	6	79.6	20.4
51–	20	5	1	0	95	5
Total	411	100	616	100	40	60

On the basis of this criterion, one can notice the differences between those involved in prostitution and those involved in procuring. Therefore, as far as prostitution is concerned, the number of perpetrators increases with age, up to the age of 29, then the numbers drop abruptly. The age category best represented is between 21 and 29.

With procurers, the situation is somewhat different. It can be noticed that up to the age of 18, a low number of perpetrators were reported as procurers. Above the age of 18, the number doubles, and at some point quadruples for those between 21 and 29. In the case of procurers, there is a steady decline after the age of 29; only after the ages of 50 do the numbers decrease significantly. The number of under age procurers may be greater, as they are the ones who usually intermediate the transaction, which therefore covers the older procurers. This could account for the drop in numbers for the registered procurers over 29 years of age, a situation that reflects more likely their ability to avoid police interference rather than their going out of business.

The prostitutes over the age of 18 represent 74 per cent of all the cases, whereas the procurers over this age represent 95 per cent of the total. Of the total number of persons over the age of 18 in this profession, 46 per cent deal in procuring and 54 per cent in actual prostitution.

Table 4: Statistical Data on Prostitution/Procuring in Relation to the Perpetrators' Occupation

Occupation	Procurers (Pc)		Prostitutes (Ps)		Proportions	
	No.	%	No.	%	Pc %	Ps %
Pupils	4	0.9	23	3.7	15	85
Students	0	0	3	0.4	0	0
Without occupation	298	72.5	556	90.2	35	65
Unemployed	1	0.2	2	0.3	33	66
Other occupations	108	26.2	32	5.1	77	23
Total	411	100	616	100	40	60

In the case of prostitution, the least represented categories are those of students and unemployed people, representing a percentage of 0.4 and 0.3 respectively of the total. Next come the pupils and those in the category 'other occupations', who make up 3.7 and 5.1 respectively of the total. The greatest weight is carried by those with no occupation, this is 90.2 per cent.

In the case of procurers, the situation is different. The students and the unemployed still hold a small percentage of the total, and the number of pupils is less than 1 per cent. Contrary to this the number of perpetrators falling in the category of 'other occupations' increases visibly; this would suggest the existence of professions declared only as a cover.

Table 5: Statistical Data on Prostitution/Procuring in Relation to the Perpetrator's Level of Education

Level of Education	Procurers (Pc)		Prostitutes (Ps)		Proportions	
	No.	%	No.	%	Pc %	Ps %
Gymnasium school	283	68	484	78.6	37	63
Technical school	24	5.8	18	2.9	66	33
High school	73	17.76	86	14	46	54
University	8	1.9	5	0.8	61	39
Unknown	23	5.5	23	3.7	46	54
Total	411	100	616	100	40	60

As far as the education level is concerned, one can notice a great resemblance between prostitutes and procurers. Those with elementary studies make up 78.6 per cent of the prostitutes and 68 per cent of the procurers, whereas those who graduated from high school or from vocational school, the ratio is different: 2.9 per cent in the case of prostitutes and 14 per cent in that of procurers, respectively, 5.8 per cent and 17.7 per cent. It is only in the case of people with higher education that the ratio changes significantly: it is 6:4 in the favour of procurers.

Table 6: Statistical Data on Prostitution/Procuring in Relation to the Perpetrators' Background

Background	Procurers (Pc)		Prostitutes (Ps)		Proportions	
	No.	**%**	**No.**	**%**	**Pc %**	**Ps %**
Rural	60	14.6	203	33	23	76
Urban	351	85.4	413	66	46	54
Total	411	100	616	100	40	60

Depending on their origin, it is noticeable that a great majority of both prostitutes and procurers come from an urban environment. In the case of prostitution, 66 per cent of the total are from an urban environment and 33 per cent from a rural environment. Combining both prostitutes and procurers, 85.4 per cent of the perpetrators are from an urban environment and 14.6 per cent from a rural environment.

International Connections of Prostitution in Romania

After 1990, Romania entered the international market of prostitution both as an importer and, more importantly, as an exporter of professionals. The number of prostitutes from abroad that practice in Romania is relatively low, and their area of origin is, in the majority of cases, the republics of the former Soviet Union. Those who occasionally practise prostitution can be found primarily in the frontier regions and the real professionals in Bucharest. On the whole, Romania is used as a stepping stone en route to other countries that offer more possibilities to 'grow professionally'.

The activity of Romanian prostitutes and procurers who practice abroad presents a more complex picture. These people can be found primarily in

Western Europe, Greece, the Near East (Turkey, Cyprus, some Arab countries), but also in more exotic places, like Malta, South Korea, Taiwan.

More commonly, in the above mentioned countries the recruitment of prostitutes is done under the cover of adverts offering jobs such as 'ballet dancers', 'exotic dancers', 'entertainers' and 'cocktail waitresses'.

Turkey was most favoured by Romanian prostitutes between 1990 and 1996. It lost attractiveness following the appearance of prostitutes from the former Soviet Union, who invaded the market and lowered the prices. Presently, the total number of prostitutes in Istanbul is approximately 10 to 15,000, this number decreasing due to the migration of professionals to the Mediterranean resorts, where it seems that they found better working conditions. This migration reached its peak in 1995 and since then has been on a steady decline. However, in Istanbul there are currently over 30 hotels catering exclusively to prostitutes and procurers.

According to the statistics, 85 per cent of the Romanian prostitutes working in Turkey between 1990 and 1995 were young divorcées, many with children, then those from dysfunctional families, (approx. 13 per cent), followed by those from the ranks of the curious and the adventurous (approx. two per cent). Romanian prostitutes in Turkey can be divided into three categories:

- Luxury (kept women): they come from Romania by plane and they have one lover, maximum 2, who pays for their stay all through their 'appointment' at a month and a half; these women receive around $2,000 on their departure from Turkey.
- Those who have 6–7 habitual customers, who come back by coach, having earned between $300 and $800.
- 'The ugly', who make up the lowest category of prostitutes, who pick up their customers in the street and who have the lowest prices. They rarely manage to put together more than $300 by the end of their stay.

The majority of Romanian procurers are gypsies (Roma), mostly with a criminal history, who associate in groups and co-operate according to the Romanian province they come from, by occupying a hotel or bed and breakfast.

It is worth noting the system of controlling this phenomenon that has been implemented by the Turkish Police. This involves organising regular raids, arresting and fining the prostitutes, taking them for medical check-ups and as a final resort expelling them from the country with an interdiction visa on their passports if they are found to be carrying a venereal disease.

Conclusion

In Romania there still appears to be no official policy that exists to provide help for those young people involved in the street sex industry, (Romanian Save The Children, 1994). However, they are now identified as a group with problems and their protection is within the general provisions for child protection. Concern for young people appears indirect, many decisions concerning them are issued on the basis of outdated laws which bear little resemblance to current social realities. Young people in the sex industry are still considered by many as delinquent. This negative outlook has to be changed, as it does globally, to contemplate preventive measures that can start to overcome this dangerous social phenomenon.

References

Adamesteanu, G. (1998). 'Desincrimination of Prostitution', interview with Mariana Stoica. *Review '22'*, August.

Alexander, P. (1980). *A Look at Prostitution*. San Francisco: National Task Force on Prostitution.

Allen, D.M. (1980). Young Male Prostitutes: Psychosocial Study. In *Archives of Sexual Behaviour*, 9(3): pp 399–426.

Botescu, G.M. (1999). *Sociogeneza conduitelor deviante in societatile de tip democratic (Sociogenesis of Deviant Behaviour in Democratic Societies)*, PhD thesis, 'Al. I. Cuza' University, Iasi, The Department of Sociology and Social Work.

Davis, N.J. (1987). Prostitution. In *Encyclopedia of Social Work*, Eighteenth Edition; Volume 2: pp 379–386. Silver Spring, Maryland: National Association of Social Workers.

Decker, J.F. (1979). *Prostitution: Regulation and Control*. Littleton, CO: Fred B. Rothman and Co.

Hart, H.L.A. (1961). *The Concept of Law*. London: Oxford University Press.

Loghin, O. and Toader, T. (1997). *Dreptul Penal Român. (Romanian Penal Law)*. Bucharest: 'Sansa' Publishing House.

Pitulescu, I. (1996). *Crima Organizata. (Organised Crime)*. Bucharest: National Publishing House.

Romanian Save the Children (1994). *Exploitation and Sexual Abuse of Street Children*.

Rosenbleet, C. and Periente, B.J. (1973). The Prostitution of the Criminal Law. In *American Law Review*, 11(3): p 373.

Rosenblum, K.E. (1975). Female Deviance and the Female Sex Role: A Preliminary Investigation. *British Journal of Sociology*, 25(1): pp 69–85.

Chapter 8

Prostitution and Young People in Russia

Svetlana Sidorenko-Stephenson

Introduction

With the beginning of reforms, Russian society has rediscovered many of the social problems that seemed to have been left far behind in the murky pre-Revolutionary past. In actual fact, of course, it was confronted with its own self, with realities that were always present but never publicly discussed. As with homelessness, drug addiction and other social problems that were depicted by the official propaganda as symptoms of capitalist degradation, prostitution had not been eradicated. It was part of a hidden agenda, that in Soviet times had been dealt with by the designated agencies of social control (militia and security forces), but largely removed from the public view.

Having resurfaced at the beginning of *perestroika*, debates about prostitution uncovered the hidden realities of Soviet society. However, prostitution very soon came to be associated with the social consequences of reforms. Since 1991, the severe economic crisis, together with the failure of the Russian state to create a robust safety net, has led to the increasing marginalisation of significant segments of the population. Growing unemployment in the formal sector of the economy has been accompanied by a rapid expansion of informal and illegal markets. Prostitution is one of the few means to survive that is open to people without significant market resources. In the face of poverty and a failure to find any legitimate means of survival, individuals are forced to get ahead by any means, including illegitimate ones, (Merton, 1957).

Low skilled working class families became particularly vulnerable from the erosion of stable institutions of work and the collapse of welfare provision. Children and young people in such families often find themselves having to fend for themselves in the streets. Others have to earn a living while staying in the family. For many young people and children, sex became their 'only saleable commodity', (c.f. McLeod, 1982), leaving them prey to exploitation by the sex industry.

This paper seeks to analyse the changes that have occurred in the general discourse on prostitution in Russia, including its legal regulation and public perceptions, and to show the changing profiles of people engaged in it. In describing how prostitution functions today, it focuses particularly on street children involved in sexual services. It concludes with a discussion of practical responses to prostitution in Russia, including prostitution among children and young people.

Prostitution in the Soviet Union—A Historical Overview

Although the Soviet State was not renowned for its liberalism and tolerance, its policies on prostitution were surprisingly liberal throughout Soviet history, especially in relation to the criminalising approach adopted by many Western countries, (Scambler *et al.*, 1990). This paradox is explained by the tradition of women's liberation which the Bolsheviks inherited from a long revolutionary tradition and which had a lasting legacy. The acceptance of free sexuality, and the recognition of women's vulnerability in the domestic sphere and in the labour market, were crucial determinants in the direction of policies applied to gender relations in Soviet Russia, (Goldman, 1993).

This approach is very obvious in the early documents adopted by the Bolsheviks, where the policies towards prostitution were set out. For example, the Decree 'On Measures to Fight Prostitution' postulated that 'the Soviet state does not want to intrude into gender relations, as any forced regulatory measures in this area can only lead to the perversion of sexual self-identification of free and economically independent citizens', (Izvestiya VTsIK, 1922). Legal regulation was only deemed necessary in cases of rape, assault on minors, in case of 'threats of parasitism', venereal disease and other socially dangerous phenomena. The two main policies applied to prostitution were prevention and prosecution. Prevention was executed through the elimination of female unemployment and children's and female homelessness, the insurance of safety of female labour and maternity and 'labour assistance to women'. New institutions were organised for these purposes, including institutes of social assistance and social patronage for homeless women. At the same time, a system of labour correction was established to deal with 'healthy women involved in prostitution or being on the verge of it'. These women were sent to labour or medical-labour colonies and factory workshops. A comprehensive system of medical and hygiene education was also established.

The measures applied to prostitutes were different. A working woman who was involved in prostitution irregularly, for example, due to poverty, would be assisted and offered education. Professional prostitutes, whose only source of income was selling sex, were treated as social parasites and deserters of labour. Other measures were aimed at prevention of demand for prostitutes and procurement. Legal punishment was introduced for clients and pimps, procurement and brothel keeping, involvement of children and women into vice, and also for the dissemination of venereal diseases by prostitutes. In the majority of cases clients were subjected to 'moral and political condemnation'. However, if they used the services of under age prostitutes, they could undergo criminal punishment. Procurers were treated in the same way.

In the 1930s, professional prostitution started to decrease. But irregular prostitution did not diminish, nor did crime against minors. In the 1930s, as unemployment was diminishing and prostitution was not, the paradigm of social control started to change. Repression against organised prostitution became a predominant form of regulation. Simultaneously, the system of social assistance and rehabilitation of women involved in sexual commerce was dismantled. The NKVD, (later KGB), became the main agency dealing with the problem, (Afanasyiev, 1998: p 158). Often this was done through recruiting prostitutes to become informers, (Shelley, 1996: p 152). Even in those harsh times no criminal or administrative punishment for prostitution was introduced. Interestingly, the toughening of policies against prostitution coincided with each attempt at reforming socialism—both with Khruschev's 'thaw' and Gorbachev's *perestroika*. As both leaders (at least initially) hoped to improve the system by fighting against those who deviated from socialist morality, prostitutes and others engaged in informal unregulated market activities became one of the targets for repression.

When the new Criminal Code of RSFSR was adopted in 1960, 'violation of passport rules', (i.e. the lack of a residence permit), became a criminal offence, (Article 198). Criminal punishment was also introduced for 'systematic vagrancy and begging' and for 'long-term parasitic way of life', (Article 209), and was up to three years imprisonment. Similar provisions were introduced into the Criminal Codes of other Soviet republics. Both articles were abolished in Russia in December 1991. Prostitutes, many of whom did not lead a settled life and lacked residence permits, housing or official employment, were often tried under these articles. Also, after coming back from prison, many of them would be unable to get their housing back. According to the Russian Housing Code, after six months of imprisonment people would lose their residency rights. This rule was only abolished in July 1995.

Other provisions in the Criminal Code dealt more specifically with prostitution-related offences: infection with a venereal disease, (Article 115 UK), evasion of medical treatment, (115-1), involvement of others into prostitution, (210), brothel keeping and procurement, (226). A mother involved in prostitution could be deprived of parental rights if it was found that she 'deviated from her responsibilities in upbringing or produced harmful effect on children by amoral and antisocial behaviour', (Article 19 of the Marriage and Family Code).

When, at the start of Gorbachev's *perestroika*, the first accounts and stories about prostitutes started to appear in newspapers and a major public reaction followed, there emerged a situation akin to that of *moral panics*, (Cohen, 1972, Goode and Ben-Yehuda, 1994). The first stories about prostitution initially raised only the subject of 'hard currency prostitutes'—those women who were selling sex to foreigners for much valued hard currency or Western clothes. The public was concerned that prostitutes would become an object of envy for many Russian women who could not afford good clothes, even less other luxuries. The glamorous image of a prostitute was reinforced by the publication of a novel 'Interdevochka' (International girl) by Vladimir Kunin. This was later turned into a film. Newspapers were full of letters by concerned readers writing about the demoralisation of the young generation, who were likely to forgo honest labour and seek high incomes in prostitution, (Diyachenko, 1991).

Criminologists and militia workers who joined the debate started to argue for criminal punishment for prostitution. But criminal punishment seemed to go too far in the general climate of Gorbachev's liberalisation, and prostitution was made an offence under the administrative law. The Decree of the Presidium of the Supreme Soviet of 29 May 1987 introduced amendments and additions to the legislation of RSFSR on the responsibility for administrative crime. A new article 164-2 established the punishment for prostitution as a warning or fine. The same crime, if committed a second time within a year, would result in a bigger fine. However, the law did not give any legal definition of prostitution and the grounds on which a person could be charged for this offence. That explains why, at the peak of the anti-prostitution campaign in 1987, of 13,526 registered crimes connected to prostitution, 80 per cent of the charges were for buying and selling things from foreigners, and only 14 per cent for prostitution itself.

The new Criminal Code of Russia adopted in 1996 did not introduce criminal punishment for prostitution. Article 249 makes it an offence to involve women in prostitution, and Article 241 makes it an offence to keep brothels. However, no legal definition of prostitution has ever been established. As a result militiamen are encountering great difficulties in determining what kind of visible signs would show that a woman is involved in prostitution and that she is to be detained and fined, (Afanasyiev, 1998: p 160).

Public Opinion on Prostitution

Before the mid 1980s the existence of prostitution in the USSR was officially denied. As poverty was not supposed to exist, prostitution as an occupation could not exist either. Some studies into prostitution were conducted by criminologists and sociologists in the 1970s–1980s, but their findings were classified.

According to Kon,

> ...*the Soviet law-enforcement bodies traditionally did not like to look at negative phenomena as having social causes; it was much safer to explain them through individual pre-dispositions. In regard to prostitution this meant that a 'prostitute' who worked for money necessarily had to be a 'whore' who was getting sexual pleasure from her labour.*

> (Kon, 1997: p 328)

Even now many Russian criminologists explain prostitution through the paradigm of 'sexual demoralisation' and 'deformation of personality'. Young people in particular are seen to be drawn into prostitution by 'proliferation of non-labour incomes which makes young people want to reach material well-being by any means', (Arsenieva, 1991: p 222).

These fears, at least at the beginning of the reforms, were supported by the results of surveys among young people. When in 1989 there was a survey among teenagers in Riga and Leningrad, hard currency prostitution appeared in a list of the ten most prestigious occupations, (Kon, 1997: p 328). Moscow high school students placed prostitutes above professors on the scale of the highest paid occupations, (Gilinsky, 1998: p 107).

Eventually, however, it has started to emerge that currency prostitutes are only a very privileged group in the profession. The majority of prostitutes are women who have much smaller incomes in roubles, many of whom work at the train stations or in the streets for very little money and at high risk. This realisation, and a general increase of tolerance towards marginal groups, may have led to changes in the perceptions and attitudes to prostitution.

The public shows a growing tolerance towards prostitution, although repressive attitudes are still very frequent. In 1989 the Russian Centre for Public Opinion Research (VCIOM) conducted a public opinion poll on attitudes to deviant and marginal groups. The same survey was replicated in 1994. The samples used in each survey (3,000 adults over 16) represented, in the first case Soviet, and in the second case Russian urban and rural populations. Table 1 shows responses to the question—'What do you think should be done with prostitutes?'.

Table 1: 'What do you Think Should be Done with Prostitutes?' (VCIOM Surveys).

	1989 %	1994 %
They should be liquidated	27	18
Isolated from society	33	23
Provided assistance	8	12
Let be as they are	17	30
Cannot choose	15	17

A significant number of respondents in 1989 chose ominously 'liquidate' and 'isolate'. However, by 1994, the share of respondents who chose repressive measures dropped significantly and the share of those who were for leaving prostitutes to be as they are, increased. It must be pointed out that by 1994, the public demonstrated less repressive attitudes than in 1989 to other marginal and deviant groups: the homeless vagrants, homosexuals, the mentally ill and drug addicts.

Younger people seem to be particularly tolerant towards prostitution. In a survey conducted by Kon in 1995 among young people from 16 to 19, the researchers asked the respondents whether they agreed or disagreed with the statement: 'Sex for money should not be condemned in a modern society'. 37 per cent of girls and 46 per cent of boys agreed, (Kon, 1997: p 335).

Organisation of Prostitution and Types of Prostitutes

It is notoriously difficult to obtain any reliable evidence on the extent and composition of prostitution anywhere in the world, (Barrett, 1995). The same is true in Russia. Classified research conducted by criminologists in the 1970s often lacked any precise methodology on sampling, research methods etc. The same, to a somewhat lesser extent, can be said about most of the more recent publications on the subject. However, even on the basis of scattered and incomplete information, it seems possible to identify important differences in the way that prostitution functioned before and since the reforms. This information suggests that the demographic composition of people involved in prostitution, its organisation and its links with organised crime have changed significantly in the last ten years.

Prostitution in the 1970s and the 1980s can be seen as primarily divided into two types. The first type was prostitution by women who used it to complement meagre official salaries. These were often married women, with children, with high educational attainment and permanently resident in the places where they lived. For example, according to one of the surveys conducted in Moscow in the mid 1970s, 23.2 per cent of prostitutes had higher and incomplete higher education, while 53.9 per cent had secondary education. In a Georgian survey conducted at the same time 7.1 per cent of the prostitutes had higher education, 66.7 per cent secondary. In Moscow 17.9 per cent of the prostitutes were married, 24 per cent divorced, and 1.5 per cent were widowed. In Georgia 8 per cent were married, 51.7 per cent divorced, and 6 per cent widowed.

As for employment status, in Moscow 15.0 per cent of the prostitutes were workers, 48.6 per cent non-manual employees, 6.4 per cent students, 0.6 per cent housewives and disabled, and 29.4 per cent did not have an official job. Among the occupations, the most frequent were shop assistants, waitresses, kindergarten workers, hairdressers, nurses, telephone operators, typists, and hotel workers. The per capita income levels of the prostitutes' families were very small, (Gilinsky, 1998: pp 111–114).

A relatively small proportion of prostitutes were migrants. In the above-mentioned Moscow survey, 78.8 per cent of prostitutes had residence permits in Moscow, 13.6 per cent in the Moscow oblast and 5.4 per cent were registered outside the region. The housing situation of the prostitutes did not differ that much from that of the general urban population: 45.6 per cent lived in flats, 2.3 per cent in their own houses, 37.1 per cent in communal flats, 4.4 per cent in hostels, 1.3 per cent rented and 9.3 per cent did not have housing, (Gilinsky: p 113). In another survey, conducted in 1987 and 1988 among prostitutes in the regional centres, 7.5 per cent were migrants, (Dyukov, 1990: p 150).

The second type was street prostitution. These were predominantly older homeless women, who could be seen as dropouts from the system of legitimate employment. They were caught in the 'revolving doors' situation of convictions for 'non-labour' incomes followed by convictions for having no residence permit or a formal job. According to a survey conducted in 1987–1988 among street prostitutes, 85.5 per cent were over 30, and 90 per cent had criminal convictions, (Dyukov, 1990: p 154). Most operated on their own at train stations.

Under age prostitution was very rare. One obvious reason for this was that street children were virtually non-existent. If a child or a young person below 18 was suspected of being a runaway from home or an institution, he or she would almost immediately be picked up by the militia and placed either back with the parents or into an institution. Also, homelessness and unemployment were not until recently a youth phenomenon. They mostly affected people with previous prison convictions, alcoholics, or those separated or divorced from their spouses and left without housing, (Sidorenko-Stephenson, 1998).

Some of the prostitution took organised forms, particularly around hotels. Top party bosses enjoyed the sexual services of women provided to them during their leisure at special saunas and holiday resorts. However, the general level of organisation of prostitution was quite low. There were no well-established links between prostitution and the criminal underworld, and none between prostitution and militiamen (apart from bribes). International prostitution was non-existent as all movement between borders was strictly controlled and regulated. Commercial agencies employing the services of prostitutes, such as massage parlours, escort agencies etc., could not exist either. Now the situation has changed dramatically, both in respect of the number and composition of prostitutes, and their organisation.

The number of prostitutes has increased visibly since the start of transition. According to the Moscow City Police Authority, about 80,000 people of various ages were involved in prostitution in the central part of Moscow in 1998. They base this estimate on the fact that 70,821 were detained for 'suspicion of being involved in prostitution' in the central district of Moscow last year. However, given the fact that police register a person each time he or she is brought into the police station, the actual figure must be at least 3 times less, (Izvestiya, 1999). Even then the figure is very impressive, if we compare it with the 13,526 prostitutes registered in 1987 in the whole of Russia.

Prostitution now involves many more young people and children than it did before the transition. According to researchers in St. Petersburg, 80 per cent of prostitutes are aged below 18. A survey of 100 Moscow prostitutes showed that 87 per cent of them were less than 25 years old. 30.3 per cent were students of vocational schools, (Zhigarev, 1998: p 240). The Head of the Russian Duma Committee on Women, Family and Youth, A. Aparina, informed her committee that in the five years to 1997, crimes connected with child pornography rose by 12 times.

An indirect indicator of the number of sexually active children can be seen in the proliferation of venereal diseases among minors. While in the last six years the rate of syphilis in Russia increased 40 times, among children under 14 it has increased 77 times, (Diyachenko and Tzimbal, 1998: p 110).

Apart from the changes in the age composition, another feature is the increase in the number of migrants among prostitutes. A recent questionnaire survey of 210 professional prostitutes in Moscow showed that 67 per cent were Russian citizens, while the rest came to Moscow from CIS countries: Ukraine, Moldova and Belarus, (ibid.: p 115). Moscow residents are a minority among the prostitutes: most of them arrived in the city from somewhere else.

The organisation of prostitution has become much more sophisticated. Prostitutes now have a complex hierarchy, territorial divisions, and highly developed support organisations, with special doctors, lawyers and security provided for them by the procurers. While prostitutes previously operated more or less on their own, now they are connected to organised crime as most urban territories are divided between various criminal groups. A prostitute who dares to violate the existing 'order' can get into serious trouble and even be killed, (Gilinsky, 1998: p 330). The Mafia groups that control prostitution can involve militia protection rings, (a so-called 'krasnaya krisha'—'red roof').

The most developed form of prostitution is linked to hotels. It is strictly controlled by criminal groups. There are also various agencies that take the forms of clubs, saunas, massage parlours, introduction agencies etc. These are widely advertised in the press. Some agencies supply women for brothels abroad. At a lower level are those prostitutes with their own flats, who have their own network of clients.

Street prostitution, increasingly comprising young girls and boys, is a rapidly expanding category in the profession. At a recent conference on child prostitution in the Baltic region, (Tallinn, September, 1998), the representatives of St. Petersburg reported that, of 5,000 street children in the city, about 150 are involved in prostitution. Many of them work with pimps, some of whom are themselves only 13–14 years old. Young girls are sold to various countries of Southern Europe at an average price of 12,000 US dollars. Many of the prostitutes are 13–14 year old homeless boys who are sold at train stations, ('Trevozhnaya statistika', *Sankt-Peterburgskiye Vedomosti*, 11th September, 1998). In Moscow in 1997, according to the information of the militia reception centre for minors, 11 per cent of the girls were brought to the centre on suspicion of being engaged in prostitution.

Street Children and Prostitution: Some Results from a Recent Survey

As street children are increasingly being recruited into prostitution, it seems important to have a closer look at the mechanisms of this recruitment. I will be discussing here some of the results of my research project, 'Street Children in Russia', which took place in 1997–1998 and was sponsored by the Ford Foundation. This survey included in-depth interviews with street children (we conducted 10 interviews, each about three hours long), focus-groups with children selected by sex and age group (four groups) and a questionnaire survey of street children in Moscow, which took place in spring-summer 1998.

The total sample in Moscow comprised 123 street children. We limited the age bracket to 7–17 years. We only interviewed children who could understand and speak Russian—which excluded non-Russian migrants from Central Asia, the Caucasus or Moldova. Some indication of the national composition of street children can be derived from the records of the militia reception centre, which show that, in the second half of 1997, 52 per cent of all the children there were from Russia. 17 per cent came to Moscow from Ukraine, ten per cent from Tajikistan, eight per cent from Moldova, three per cent from Azerbaijan and three per cent from Uzbekistan. Belorussia, Georgia, Turkmenistan, Kazakhstan, Latvia, Lithuania, Kirgizstan were places of origin for seven per cent of children—about one per cent from each of these ex-USSR states. Most of the interviews took place in agencies—in the militia receptions centre (67) and shelters (24). 32 interviews were taken in the streets. For interviews that were conducted in organisations we used age and sex quotas, based on the registration of all the children who passed through militia reception centre in 1997. In the streets we used a random sample. The majority of the interviewees—72 per cent—were boys.

According to the results of our survey (based on counting children in the streets and in lofts/cellars in two districts of Moscow and then extrapolating the results to the whole of the city territory), there were about 800 genuinely homeless children living in the streets of Moscow in the summer of 1998 and up to 4,000 more were periodically sleeping at home but spending most of their time in the streets. No reliable data exists on the number of children deprived of parental care and living and/or working in the streets in the whole of Russia. Indirect indicators, however, confirm that these numbers are growing. Compared to 1988, the number of children brought from the streets to special militia reception centres in 1998 doubled. The growing numbers of children deprived of parental care led to the expansion of children's homes in Russia. In the last two years alone, the number of large state homes for so-called 'social orphans' has doubled, reaching about 1,000, and there are plans to build many more.

Young children leaving home and surviving in the streets are often seen as deviants who were allowed to become 'disaffiliated' because of the collapse of social control over young people exercised under the Soviet regime through school, after school classes, pioneer and komsomol organisations and young pioneer holiday camps. Yet the survey showed that their decisions in many cases were motivated by the desire to become affiliated to other individuals or groups rather than their families, and the collapse of Soviet youth institutions is of relatively minor relevance here, (c.f. Jones, 1997).

In our sample, 65 per cent of children ended up on the streets because they left home. Most of the children we interviewed came from so-called 'problem families', many of them single parent or reconstituted families, with a high rate of alcohol abuse and a record of problems with the law.

The composition of the families from which the street children came was surprisingly similar to that in the 1920s, when Russia also had a vast problem with homeless and neglected children, the so-called *besprizorniki*. In the 1920s, single-parent families produced a high share of *besprizorniki*. 28 per cent of the *besprizorniki* in Moscow in 1924 had only a mother, 7 per cent only a father. Only 24 per cent came from homes with both parents, (Goldman, 1993: p 80). Our data shows striking similarities with 1924 data as far as single parents are concerned: 28 per cent of the children come from families with single mothers, and 7 per cent from families with single fathers. Both now and then, such families found it very difficult to care for their children in a period of high unemployment and low wages.

Our survey showed that, as a rule, the parents of street children occupy the lowest positions on the social scale. These are predominantly unqualified manual workers, both urban and rural. Urban dwellers are a majority—about 85 per cent in the sample. These were the families that were hit hardest by the collapse of state welfare and unemployment. Most of the parents were unemployed, had casual/seasonal jobs, or begged.

Answering the question, 'Does either of your parents consume alcohol often and in large quantities?', 71.7 per cent of those interviewed answered positively. 69.1 per cent of children reported that members of their family had been in trouble with the militia. 39.8 per cent reported that one or more family members had been convicted in the past. 80 per cent of the children experienced physical violence.

By running away, children hope to be able to settle with their friends, find new families, or new opportunities in the city. Their behaviour shows a range of motives typical in migration behaviour. In this they are similar, in their choices and destinies, to other urban migrants.

For a substantial number of children, however, the choice of having to survive in the streets was made, sometimes inadvertently, by their parents. Family migration resulting in homelessness, or migration with homeless parents, comprises about 15 per cent of all cases.

In the urban jungle, the homeless children join other groups looking for a means of survival—migrants, homeless adults, and generally those people who are looking to finding new sources of living in the informal economy. Like the rest, they attempt to get incorporated into the structures that have emerged in the informal economy: trade in the informal markets, organised crime and prostitution. Some attempt to be incorporated into the sub-cultural groups such as the 'Arbat' system in Moscow.

Prostitution seems to be a way to earn a living for those children who have not been able to find more legitimate ways of earning or enjoying positive affiliations. The share drawn into professional prostitution or having to sell sex from time to time is quite substantial. In our sample, 7 out of 35 girls interviewed admitted being involved in prostitution during their life in the streets. According to many accounts, boys are also involved in prostitution, but only one of our male respondents admitted this.

There are various ways into prostitution. Some children and young people are initially coerced into prostitution by their parents or other people who have control over them. They often attempt to escape by running away—only to discover that prostitution is the only way to survive on their own. 'Olesya', a 17-year-old girl from Moldova, described a series of misfortunes that had led her into prostitution.

Three years ago, Olesya's parents, after being made redundant, decided to start their own business. In order to get initial capital, they borrowed money from several people they knew in town. But their business was not successful and angry lenders started demanding money back. In what has become a typical scenario, the family escaped and started moving from town to town trying to earn money. All the roads to prosperity led to Moscow, and the family eventually settled in a Moscow suburb. After a short period of employment with a Turkish construction company, Olesya and her parents tried to earn money selling fruit and vegetables at the market, but the earnings were barely enough to feed themselves, not to mention the other six younger children in the family. In the meantime, relations in the family deteriorated. The parents started to drink heavily. There were constant quarrels and fights. The younger children were hungry and neglected. Finally, the parents started to force Olesya to engage in prostitution with the Turkish workers from the company where they used to work. She decided to leave home and went to live at the train station. Like many of the homeless girls, she at first tried to find young men with whom she could stay for some time, but this was a precarious existence. So when she was approached by a woman in the Metro, who asked whether she would like to work as a prostitute, Olesya agreed. Now she lives in a flat with several other under age girls and works for a '*mamochka*'—a 'madam'. She feels that this is the only way for her to survive.

Other children are deceived by strangers or forced to work as prostitutes. 15-year old 'Lyuba' ran away from home and started to work in a small-town market in Moldova. There she was approached by gypsies who promised to take her to Moscow where she would earn ten thousand dollars per month. The naïve girl believed them. On arrival in Moscow she was put in a flat with other under age girls and told that she would be working as a prostitute, but on her first working day, when the girls were brought to an underground station where they had to meet clients, Lyuba escaped. After a period roaming the streets of Moscow she was brought in by the police. Other girls who were there offered to help her earn a living—again through prostitution. Now she rents a room and sells sex to people she finds in the street.

Some children get into prostitution after a period of homelessness, having tried other ways of earning a living. 'Elena', another runaway girl from Minsk, decided to approach a prostitution agency after she realised that she could no longer live with her friend's parents whom she helped with housework. Her attempts to stay with her Moscow friends from the hippy community also proved futile in the long run. As the agency suggested providing accommodation, she agreed.

Some of the others girls we interviewed—runaway girls from small towns—decided to get into prostitution as a way of starting new lives in Moscow and avoiding the dull provincial life. Theirs was a conscious decision, which, in their eyes, would ideally lead to a career as a madam in the future, when they could save money and acquire the connections with the 'right people' in the Mafia and militia.

Although prostitution is certainly a dangerous occupation, exploitative of young people, for many of the street children in a situation of complete destitution, it provides relative protection and stability. Many of them plan to leave prostitution after having saved money or becoming madams. However, they think that at the moment this is the best alternative for them.

Many of the girls interviewed talked about a state of *'bespredel'* in the society. This word, born in Soviet prisons, means a lack of any rules and norms.

> *There is such a* bespredel *in life now, I do not know how some people survive in such a system. This is terribly depressing for a human being. Physically I am very strong, I can do everything, I can work anywhere, I easily come into contact with people, but morally I am dead. Now all the professors who finished colleges, they are all trading in the market, work in business. Nobody pays wages anymore. I have nothing else to do. Where would I live if I did not work for my madam? Who would feed me?*

('Olesya')

'Bespredel', a complete normlessness (anomie in sociological terms— Durkheim, 1952), is the worst state of affairs for individuals. That is why in circumstances where people are left to fend for themselves and have no recourse to social protection, they start to look around for any possible affiliations, which they can find in organised prostitution.

As one of the underage prostitutes explained,

> *We have our own system, similar, for example, to a system in prison or a system at the market, where there is a boss who comes and collects money. The same system exists here, you are protected for nobody to bother you, for you to stand quietly and work*

('Elena').

Recruitment into prostitution happens through friends or advertisements in newspapers. For example, 'Moskovski Komsomolets', a relatively reputable newspaper, regularly publishes dozens of adverts inviting 'girls for work', (sometimes with accommodation provided). A madam rents a flat for several girls. There is 'protection'—security provided by the militia or the Mafia. If a girl is taken to a militia station, the madam comes and buys her out. The sale of the girls normally occurs near the Metro stations in central Moscow, where they wait in a car to be shown to a potential client, or in a subway to be summoned upstairs.

Some young people do not manage to enter organised prostitution. They are in a much worse position. As one of the girls told us about her cousin who worked at a train station, 'not only do they work for peanuts, there is no protection there. They have such pimps, that they (the prostitutes) have to pay (bribes in case of trouble with militia) from their own pocket, the pimps would not do it.'

Other young people are themselves involved in procurement. One of our respondents, a 14-year-old boy, has been engaged in this business for some time. He supplies young girls to clients and takes 20 per cent of the price. When he grows up he wants to be a businessman. He plans to leave pimping— this is, in his words, 'just a childhood activity'! However, despite the intention to have a more legitimate occupation in the future, he also pays a share of his money to 'zona', a collective term for inmates in prisons and penal colonies. This is not a racket, but insurance—he provides for being in the good books with the members of organised crime.

Conclusion: Prostitution and Policy Measures

The emergence of urban marginality in Russia is an essential feature of transition. As Robert Park argued, marginality is one of the most important features of urbanism. Marginality is easily tolerated in a city, where there is more crime, homelessness and prostitution, (Park, 1928). In this respect, Russian cities since the beginning of the reform process have started to look similar to those in the West, (Szelenyi, 1996: p 302).

However, the problems experienced by vulnerable groups struggling for survival are made much worse by a serious lack of opportunities for legitimate employment and the absence of facilities for rehabilitation. This is particularly true in the case of children and young people.

The system of child care in Russia is still very undeveloped, and in the majority of Russian regions a children's home continues to be the main institution where children are put when they are orphaned or their parents are deprived of parental rights. Conditions in these institutions are very severe. According to NAN, an NGO, working with street children, more than 200,000 children run away each year from state homes, from schools for delinquent children and from homes for children with mental and nervous conditions. In a December 1998 special report, 'Abandoned to the State: Cruelty and Neglect in Russian Orphanages', the human rights non-governmental organisation (NGO) Human Rights Watch exposed the severe lack of facilities for rehabilitation or socialisation of children in such institutions.

Child refugees and forced migrants find themselves completely outside the system of social protection. According to the Federal Migration Service, the number of such children in Russia has reached 300,000. According to the existing legislation, a child cannot be granted refugee status and has to be sent back to the place where he came from. Also, in Moscow, children who have no residence permit in the area are not allowed by the city authorities to be accepted into schools. They have no rights to health care either, apart from emergency hospital treatment.

The system of shelters for children is still rudimentary. In 1992 the first shelter, belonging to NAN, opened in Moscow. Now in Moscow there are also 12 municipal shelters, which each accommodates about 30 children, and several small shelters run by NGOs. According to the regulations of the city authorities, these shelters can only accept children who have a Moscow residence permit. Children who are not registered in the given place can only go to a militia reception centre. The militia has to investigate, within a 30 day period, whether a child has committed a crime or run away from an institution. If neither condition applies, and he or she has a home, they will be sent back home regardless of the circumstances. If a girl or a boy has been involved in prostitution, the reception centre notifies the local militia department at the place of the young person's residence.

No special organisations or provisions exist, either on the state level, or in the voluntary sector, to assist those minors who engage in prostitution. Special 'vice squads', organised by the militia, are understaffed, and in St. Petersburg, for example, this department comprises four people. Periodic campaigns against corrupt militiamen who take bribes from prostitutes, or demand sex, do not seem to have any effect.

Policing prostitution has had the same corrupting impact on police as it has had in other countries, (e.g. the United States). Not only does the militia fail to deter or reform prostitutes, their enforcement of laws prohibiting prostitution has aggravated corruption within the law enforcement body, (Shelley, 1996: p 153). All of the under age prostitutes we interviewed in our survey cited one or more instances of being stopped in the streets by militia who demanded either bribes or sex. The threat was that they would otherwise be sent to the militia reception centre, where the children are locked up for 30 days while the militia checks their background. Some of the girls were involved in organised prostitution where a specific militia station provided 'protection' against organised crime or problems with clients.

Although the main thrust of the current legislation seems to be to prevent people, especially minors, from becoming involved in prostitution, this work has been very ineffective. For example, by 1995 the Petersburg Department on the Control of Prostitution and Pornography had information on about 160 procurement agencies. However, of 28 criminal proceedings against brothel keeping and procurement that were instituted in St. Petersburg in 1994, only one was brought to court, and a suspended sentence was given. The militia personnel explain that the lack of success is a result of withdrawal of evidence by witnesses, (Afanasiev, 1998: p 163).

Although protection of children involved in prostitution is extremely important, the key to solving the problem is prevention. The answer to the proliferation of children's and young people's involvement in prostitution is the development of a childcare system, in particular foster care and prevention of child abuse and neglect, and NGO facilities that will work with children at risk. There has been some progress in this area lately. UNICEF and the Ministry of Labour and Social Development are conducting a joint experiment to establish regional Children's Ombudsmen. The Samara region is rapidly developing a system of foster care (in January 1999, 500 of the 876 foster families in Russia were in Samara). Fifteen regions of Russia have created adoption centres. A number of NGOs have created shelters and day centres for street children. Although these are only the first steps, it is impossible to prevent the exploitation of children and young people without creating a robust system that would accommodate children who are not supported by their families and who run away from institutions.

As for prostitution in general, there is still a lot of discussion on the most appropriate policies. The 'liberals', including some progressive criminologists and sociologists of gender, have become the most vocal camp in the debate. They argue that the introduction of criminal punishment cannot be effective. They insist on economic measures and education and say that criminal punishment should only exist for the proliferation of prostitution. The 'radicals' want to legalise prostitution and to make prostitutes pay taxes and receive medical help. This position has even found official support in the region of Saratov, where the regional Ombudsman has persuaded the governor to develop a project on legalising brothels.

The Moscow authorities have considered creating zones of tolerance where prostitution can take place. One such attempt—aborted because of the protests of the locals—took place on the eve of the Children's Goodwill Games in July, 1998. However, there are immense problems with the legal justification for moving prostitutes from one area of the city into another, (Kon, 1997: p 336).

Some still argue for criminal punishment for prostitution. They claim that prostitution is morally pernicious for society, it undermines marriage, breeds venereal disease and AIDS, and is connected with crime. 'A favourite Soviet motive—"the gaining of non-labour incomes" has now given way to "the vice of lechery" ', (ibid.: p 335). This position is associated with the new 'pro-life' movement, which has emerged in Russia in the last several years. It is supported by the nationalist and conservative political camps. 'Sexual demoralisation', in the eyes of the proponents of this movement, came to be linked to an opportunity to buy condoms, effective ways of the treatment of venereal disease, availability of medical abortion, moral and material support to single mothers and premarital sex. The recent failure of a UNESCO sponsored programme to introduce sex education into schools is an outcome of the victory of this camp, supported by the State Duma Committee on Family, Women and Youth, over their opponents in the Ministry of Health and the Ministry of Education. A very successful network of family planning centres is currently deprived of state funding due to opposition in the State Duma. The solution to the 'sexual demoralisation' of young people is seen through a 'propaganda of spiritual values'.

The days when propaganda could have any success are, however, over. 'Losers' in the transition, including an ever increasing number of young people, will have to find some means of survival. Many of them will inevitably be breaking social and legal conventions and be drawn into dangerous and exploitative occupations, including prostitution. The situation demands both a credible long term strategy for social policy reform and immediate short term solutions if these young people are not to find themselves permanently excluded from society.

References

Afanasyiev, V. (1998). Socialniy kontrol za prostitutsiyei v Rossii. (Social Control over Prostitution in Russia). In Gilinsky, Ya.I. (Ed.). *Sotsialnyi control nad deviantnim povedeniyem v sovremennoi Rossii*, pp 144–164. St. Petersburg: St. Petersburgskiy filial Instituta sotsiologii RAN, Baltiisky institut ekologii, politiki, prava.

Arsenieva, M.I. (1991). Istoki polovoi demoralizatsii molodyozhi. (The Sources of Sexual Demoralisation of Youth). In *Prostitutsiya i prestupnost*, pp 210–230. Moscow: Yuridicheskaya literatura.

Barrett, D. (1995). Child Prostitution. *Highlight*, No. 135. National Children's Bureau.

Cohen, S. (1972). *Folk Devils and Moral Panics; The Creation of the Mods and Rockers*. London: McGibbon and Kee.

Diyachenko, A.P. (1991). Interdevochki v zerkale pressi. (Hard Currency Prostitutes in the Mirror of the Press). In *Prostitutsiya i prestupnost*, pp 71–98.

Diyachenko, A.P. and Tzimbal, Ye. (1998). Sotsialniy kontrol za deviantnim sexualnim povdeniyem. (Social Control over Deviant Sexual Behaviour). In Gilinsky, Ya.I. (Ed.). *Sotsialnyi control nad deviantnim povedeniyem v sovremennoi Rossii*, pp 110–118.

Durkheim, E. (1952). *Suicide: A Study in Sociology*, (first published 1912). London: Routledge and Kegan Paul.

Dyukov, V.V. (1990). Grimasi rinka svobodnoi lyubvi. (The Grimaces of the 'Free-love' Market). In *Prostitutsiya i prestupnost*, pp 148–162.

Fedorovskiy, A.N. (1928). Sovremennaya prostitutisya (Opit sotsialno-gigiyenicheskogo issledovaniya). (Modern Prostitution. An attempt at Socio-hygienic Research). *Profilakticheskaya medicina*, pp 9–10.

Gabiani, A.A. and Manuilskiy, M.A. (1987). Cena lyubvi (Obsledovaniye prostitutok v Gruzii). (The Cost of Love. A Survey of Georgian Prostitutes). *Sociologicheskiye issledovaniy*a, 6: pp 61–68.

Gilinsky, Ya.I. (1998). Prostitutsiya kak ona est. (Prostitution as it is). In *Prostitutsiya i prestupnost*, pp 99–122.

Goldman, W.Z. (1993). *Women, the State and the Revolution: Soviet Family Policy and Social Life, 1917–1933.* Cambridge University Press

Goode, E. and Ben-Yehuda, N. (1994). *Moral Panics: The Social Construction of Deviance.* Cambridge, MA. and Oxford: Blackwell.

Human Rights Watch (1998). *Abandoned to the State: Cruelty and Neglect in Russian Orphanages.*

Izvestiya VTsIK, 16th December, 1922.

Izvestiya, Moskva Stala Gorodom Krasikh Fonarei, 17th March, 1999.

Jones, J. Youth Homelessness and the 'Underclass'. In Macdonald, R. (Ed.). *Youth, the 'Underclass' and Social Exclusion.* London: Routledge.

Kon, I.S. (1997). *Seksualnaya clutura v Rossii. Klubnichka na berezke.* (The Sex Culture in Russia. A Strawberry on a Birch Tree). Moscow: OGI.

Levada, Yu.A. (1995). Chelovek sovetskiy: pyat let spustya: 1989–1994 (predvaritelniye itogi sravnitelnogo issledovaniya). (A Soviet Person in Five Years: 1989–1994 (preliminary results of a comparative survey)). *Informatsionniy Bulleten Monitoringa*, 1–2: p 10.

Merton, R. (1957). *Social Theory and Social Structure.* Glencoe: Free Press.

McLeod, E. (1982). *Women Working: Prostitution Now.* London: Croom Helm.

Park, R.E. (1928). Human Migration and the Marginal Man. *American Journal of Sociology*, 33: pp 881–893.

Szelenyi, I. (1996). Cities Under Socialism—and After. In Andrusz, G., Harloe, M. and Szelenyi, I. (Eds.). *Cities after Socialism. Urban and Regional Change and Conflict in Post-socialist Societies.* Oxford and Cambridge, MA: Blackwell.

Scambler, G., Peswani, R., Renton, A. and Scambler, A. (1990). Women Prostitutes in the AIDS Era. *Sociology of Health and Illness*, 12: pp 260–273.

Sidorenko-Stephenson, S. (1998). *The Russian Homeless: Old Problem, New Agenda.* Paper presented at the Annual BASEES conference, Cambridge, April 1998.

Shelley, L.I. (1996). *Policing Soviet Society: The Evolution of State Control.* London: Routledge.

Zhigarev, V. (1998). Na grebne sexualnoi volni. (At the Top of the Sex Wave). *Prostititsiya i prestupnost*, pp 230–254.

Chapter 9

Child Prostitution: A Scottish Perspective

Robert Buckley and Stewart B. Brodie

Introduction

In this chapter we will provide an outline of the criminal justice system in Scotland and its overlap with the Scottish Child Care System, in an effort to examine why the recognition of child prostitution has been impeded. It is also important to acknowledge and appreciate that there is a very separate and distinct legal system within Scotland. We will therefore provide an overview of legislation and its application to the child welfare and criminal justice systems. Finally, we will discuss how the problem is being tackled from a practitioner's point of view, highlighting the very real concerns that exist in this field.

Policy Context

Throughout history the discovery, acknowledgement and acceptance of child-centred social problems, has been a difficult and turbulent process. Writers such as Corby, (1993), have stressed the societal and professional hurdles that the work of Kempe and Kempe, (1978), and Finklehor, (1986), has had to overcome in gaining recognition of physical abuse and sexual abuse of children as serious social issues. In some respects, the identification of child prostitution could be said to be experiencing similar obstacles of recognition. The heightened awareness and growing concern about child prostitution within some professionals and policy makers has been acknowledged, (Barrett, 1997). On the other hand, it is not an exaggeration to state that the subject has yet to claim the minds and attention of the majority of politicians, police, health services, social workers, the media and perhaps more significantly the general public. This is despite the Home Office figures for 1998 showing that the number of children aged 17 and under prosecuted for prostitution rose from 101 in 1995 to 219 in 1996, with another 287 receiving cautions during that same year, (BBC News, 29th January, 1998). In researching child prostitution in Scotland, it became clear that the issue has been slow to evolve as a major source of concern. One significant explanation is with the nature and operation of the child justice/welfare system and how we process referrals to the Children's Reporter and the Children's Hearing System. On the other hand, unlike England and Wales, where the issue has received some attention, to date there has been very little written on the subject in Scotland, (Barrett ,1997). One simplistic, if somewhat complacent explanation, is that in keeping with the wider United Kingdom perspective, child prostitution has been largely overlooked by practitioners, researchers, and policy makers. An illustration of this is that in 1998 the Scottish Office published the Children's Safeguard Review. The report focused on a wide range of child care topics such as abuse, residential care provision, children's rights and after care provision, and it was the first official report to focus on child protection as an issue. The report commented, however, that 'there is very little literature and research on child prostitution in the UK'.

On a practice level, there are a number of projects, particularly within the Glasgow and Edinburgh area, that deal with the problem on a daily basis. The slow recognition of the potential scale of the problem is worrying, given the estimated number of under age prostitutes known to be operating. In Glasgow recently, the estimated number of working prostitutes was suggested as being 1,000. Perhaps more significantly, 10 per cent of these women are believed to have started prostitution before the age of 16, (BBC Scotland, 16th January, 1999).

The Criminal Law and Offences

The Civic Government (Scotland) Act, 1982, is the key legislation with regard to prostitution in Scotland. Under Section 46, there are two specific offences. Prosecutions are classified in terms of contravention of this section.

Firstly, there is the offence of 'loitering with intent', which makes it an offence for a prostitute to linger on the street with the intention of offering their services for sale. This is normally dealt with by means of an informal police warning, often without the formality of an arrest.

The second, and most common offence, is that of 'soliciting', where a prostitute approaches a person offering their services for sale. This offence is also considered in terms of being a contravention of Section 46 of the Civic Government (Scotland) Act, 1982, and would be dealt with by the local district court. If a person under the age of 16 was apprehended for these offences, the matter would be considered from a perspective of the young person's welfare and a report would be sent to the Children's Reporter. The Children's Reporter would then investigate the case as to whether the child's welfare was compromised, given that they have a specific duty that the child's welfare is a paramount consideration in terms of Section 11 of the Children Act (Scotland), 1995. Depending on the circumstances and the degree of risk, the police could consider applying under Section 63 of the Children (Scotland) Act, 1995, for the child or young person to be detained in a place of safety pending the Reporter's investigation of the case. In such cases, the child or young person must appear before a children's hearing within three days.

Recently the Criminal Law (Consolidation) Act, 1995, was introduced and brought together a range of offences under the one Act. With regard to prostitution, this Act defines a series of offences for a person procuring the services of a prostitute. More specifically, with regard to child prostitution, it makes it a specific offence for an adult to procure the services of a girl aged between 13 and 16 years.

Finally, it is worth noting that unlike England and Wales, where 'kerb crawling' is a specific offence in terms of being a contravention of either Section 1 or Section 2 of the Sexual Offences Act, 1985, in Scotland such offences would often receive an informal warning by the police. Those prosecuted for 'kerb crawling' would be dealt with under the common law offence or breach of the peace.

The Criminal Justice System

The Scottish criminal justice system has a three-tier procedure for processing offences and dispensing justice, (Manson-Smith, 1995).

The District Court: This is the lowest court, which deals with minor offences. It has limited sentencing powers of up to 60 days imprisonment and/or the imposition of a fine of up to £2,500. It is in this court that many offences of soliciting are dealt with. The court is presided over by a local Justice of the Peace. The exception to this is in Glasgow, where there are also stipendiary magistrates, who are legally qualified and have the same sentencing powers as a Sheriff in summary proceedings.

The Sheriff Court: This court deals with the majority of crime. It is presided over by a legally qualified judge known as the Sheriff. In summary proceedings a Sheriff exclusively hears the cases and sentencing powers are limited to three months imprisonment or a fine of up to £5,000. In solemn proceedings, i.e. more serious cases, the case is tried before a Sheriff and jury and the sentencing powers are up to three years imprisonment, with no limit on the amount of a fine that can be imposed.

The High Court: This considers the most serious criminal acts such as murder, attempted murder and rape.

Following the arrest of any person who is then charged with a criminal offence, the police will prepare a report for the Procurator Fiscal's Office. This service provides the same function as the Crown Prosecution Service in England and Wales. The Procurator Fiscal will set the date for court and prepare the prosecution evidence.

If the person charged with an offence is under 16 years, the Procurator Fiscal sends a report on the offence to the local Children's Reporter. They will investigate the child's circumstances in terms of the Children (Scotland) Act 1995 and whether the child requires compulsory measures of supervision. This brings the case within the jurisdiction of the children's hearing system. There are some exceptions to this rule:

- Where a person under 16 has been charged in conjunction with an adult, then both accused have to be treated via the same system, that of the criminal proceedings with the Sheriff Court.
- Where the young person has been charged with a very serious crime that normally falls within the remit of the High Court.

Young people aged between 16 and 18 are dealt with as adults by the criminal justice system. Therefore, the majority of young people arrested for prostitution or any other offence would be dealt with by the district courts. If, however, a person between 16 and 18 was arrested for an offence and was still under the supervision of the children's hearing system, the case would be referred back to the children's hearing for consideration, as opposed to going to court. This is a good illustration of legislation ensuring that the welfarism ethos of the children's hearing system interfaces with the criminal justice system.

In some cases the Procurator Fiscal may make use of the diversion programme, which strives to keep first offenders out of the court system. With their agreement, the Procurator Fiscal can decide to refer a young person, or indeed anyone, to their local authority social work department for advice, counselling and support. This is a preventative strategy and could be used if, in the view of the Procurator Fiscal, the welfare needs of the young person outweigh the demands of the criminal justice system. Diversion, however, is a one-off attempt to prevent conviction and is activated solely at the discretion of the Procurator Fiscal. At first glance diversion appears an innovative and progressive option, but the development and operation of the programme has been inconsistent throughout the country.

Child Care Legislation

The central legislation in Scotland is the Children (Scotland) Act, 1995. This legislation came into force in two stages. The first stage was in October, 1996, with the second stage following in April, 1997. In many respects this legislation is not dissimilar from the 1989 Children Act for England and Wales, in that it shares much of the same terminology and concepts such as, 'children in need', 'accommodation' and 'looked after children'. Perhaps more importantly it is underpinned by the same philosophical thinking in terms of seeking to locate social work with children and families within a spirit of partnership.

The Children's Reporter

This is the agency responsible for the co-ordination of legal action concerning children who may be at risk, or are vulnerable for a variety of reasons. The Children's Reporter has a central administration in Stirling, which is concerned with the monitoring of quality assurance and policy development of the service. Operational aspects of the service are devolved to the local Children's Reporters, whose jurisdiction coincides with the various Local Authorities. Their role is the co-ordination of the legal processes concerning children up to the age of 16 who may be in need of compulsory measures of supervision.

The Reporter has a statutory duty under Section 56 of the Children (Scotland) Act, 1995 to investigate situations concerning children. There are a range of specific areas of concern on which the Reporter may act, known as the 'grounds of referral', and are defined under Section 52 (2) of the 1995 Act. They include such diverse concerns as failing to attend school regularly, being the victim of a Schedule 1 offence, being without parental control and being in moral danger. The grounds also include situations where a child has committed an offence.

The Scottish Child Care System

The child care system in Scotland has a strong tradition of integrating practice with regard to child welfare and children who commit offences. The children's hearing system has been in operation since 1971 and has strived to maintain a focus of children's welfare in dealing with a wide range of child centred problems of which the committing of offences is but one aspect of behaviour.

In response to a referral of a child, the Reporter has a duty to make enquiries and call for reports from a variety of sources, particularly from the child's school and the local social work department. He will then draw up specific grounds of referral on which basis the child will come before a children's hearing where the case will be discussed by the children's panel.

A decision is made by the children's panel, which is a tribunal of three lay people who can decide to place the child on supervision to the local authority either at home, in foster care, in residential care or a particular specialist resource. The panel may also request additional reports from child welfare professionals. It is important to note that the hearing is the actual process and the panel is the group of people who make the decision. The role of the Reporter is to oversee the legalities of the hearing process and to ensure that the panel makes decisions that are legally competent. The hearing process works on a consensus basis and proceeds to a conclusion only if the grounds of referral are accepted by the parents and the child. In contested cases the hearing has to refer the case to the Sheriff Court for the grounds of referral to be proven or 'established'. As the grounds of referral are formulated under civil law proceedings, the standard of proof is that of a 'balance of probabilities'. The exception to this is if the child has committed an offence, then the standard of proof has to be the higher criminal standard of 'beyond reasonable doubt'. This is to guarantee children the same civil liberties as adults in determining if they committed an offence.

The following stages all come under the Children (Scotland) Act, 1995.

Stage 1
Police, family, school, social work, or indeed any person can refer a child to the Children's Reporter.

Stage 2
The Reporter requests an initial investigation report from the local authority social work and the child's school. They may also make inquiries with other agencies or people depending on the nature of the case. At this stage the process is very much inquisitorial.

Stage 3
The Reporter assesses evidence and the need for the child to be subject to compulsory measures of care, having regard to the fact that under Section 11, the child's welfare is paramount.

Stage 4

The Reporter formulates specific grounds of referral in keeping with the criteria set out in Section 52 (2) of the Act. The grounds of referral are accompanied by a supporting statement of facts.

Stage 5a

The Reporter arranges a children's hearing where the children's panel consider the case. If the child and family accept the grounds of referral then discussion can take place. The panel can decide that the child needs compulsory measures of supervision under Section 70 of the Act.

Stage 5b

If grounds are denied or disputed then the case has to go before the local Sheriff Court for consideration.

Stage 5c

If the grounds are not established the case will be dismissed. Where grounds are established by the Sheriff, the case is remitted back to the children's hearing system for the panel to make the appropriate disposal. At this point the panel can decide that the child needs compulsory measures of supervision under Section 70 of the Act.

The most distinctive feature of the hearing system is that it does not differentiate between children who have committed offences and those who are placed on supervision for reasons of their own welfare or protection. Over the years there have been attempts to impose a more judicial and punitive approach, but this has been effectively resisted, (Tisdall, 1998). There is not the equivalent of the range of sentencing options open to juvenile courts highlighted by Braye and Preston, (1997). They argue that the Criminal Justice and Public Order Act 1994 very much places youth crime within the juvenile justice arena. In effect it means the panel does not differentiate offenders from non-offenders in their decision making process, although for the purposes of the Rehabilitation of Offenders Act 1974, a disposal from a children's hearing for an offence ground of referral is recorded as a criminal conviction. The integration in approach to both offenders and non-offenders in terms of disposal of a case, is the cornerstone of the philosophy of welfarism that underpins the children's hearing system in operation. It does mean in practice, however, that because there is no linking of disposals to specific offences, estimating the incidence of prostitution through the hearing system is virtually impossible.

The classification of referrals to the Reporter may have a crucial role in the failure of the system to pick up on the incidence of child prostitution within

Scotland. Figures for 1995 show that the number of children who were referred to the Reporter was 42,924, of which 59 per cent were in respect of children who had committed offences, (Scottish Office, 1995: Section 52). Whilst official figures do break down the category of the offences, this classification of offences is not sufficiently specific to identify prostitution. Therefore, it is impossible to ascertain the number of under 16s who are apprehended by the police for child prostitution.

A further complication is that some children involved in child prostitution may be dealt with under Section 52(2) of the Children (Scotland) Act as being 'in moral danger'. This response has advantages in that it does not criminalise the child or young person, but still accesses them to the child welfare system for supervision and intervention. Another possible advantage of cases being dealt with via this legal process is that in potentially controversial proceedings, the contested grounds would be proven to the standard of the balance of probabilities and the focus is more concerned with the young person's welfare as opposed to their culpability or guilt within criminally driven proceedings. In practice, this option may prove easier in gathering evidence that supports a view that a child is in moral danger, as opposed to establishing their involvement in specific criminal activity.

On the other hand, although there are figures cited annually for children considered to be in moral danger, they do not assist in establishing the extent or any estimate of the incidence of child prostitution. This is because the consolidated figure contains various dangerous situations for children, of which child prostitution may be only one aspect.

The Practice Context

Prostitution has been well documented as an international phenomenon for thousands of years. Lujo Basserman's *The Oldest Profession*, (1967), provides a detailed history of prostitution. In the main, the fact that prostitution takes place is generally known to most of the adult population even if the actual sexual act takes place behind closed doors. In Scotland today, the knowledge that women and perhaps to a lesser extent adult men do provide sexual services is within the public domain. The murder of seven female prostitutes in the last five years in Glasgow and the subsequent press reporting of these crimes has contributed to public awareness of prostitution on its own doorstep. It remains likely, however, that apart from those professionals who have regular contact, the details of the working lives of prostitutes is generally less well known.

There are a number of reasons why prostitution remains clandestine. Prostitution is a dangerous activity, a criminal offence and a form of work that attracts little status from a generally hostile public. In addition, the illegal use of drugs has a high usage rate amongst adult prostitutes. These two factors together generate the need for a low profile activity, although it is generally accepted that prostitution by adult men and adult women does take place. The situation with regard to child prostitution is very different in terms of public awareness and recognition. This very much mirrors professional acknowledgement and appreciation of child prostitution as a serious social issue.

One agency that has kept records that assist in providing an indication of the numbers of young women involved in prostitution, is the City Centre Initiative in Glasgow. This project offers a range of advice and support services to women involved in prostitution.

The City Centre Initiative (CCI) was established in 1991. From its inception, the project has been developed using streetwork as a primary means of identifying vulnerable young people within the city centre and then endeavouring to establish and maintain contact with this group. At present, CCI's street team of six staff operates five nights per week, Sunday to Thursday, between 6.00 pm and 2 am. Street workers operate in pairs and normally cover the main city centre areas, focusing time and effort on the bus and train stations as well as the main street prostitution areas. Street work allows CCI to contact young people who are most isolated and who for various reasons feel unable to make use of other supports, many of which may only operate during normal working hours.

CCI carry out a number of important roles in their work with young people:

- Acting as a safety net to the most isolated young people in the city centre by initiating and maintaining contact.
- Linking young people in to supports available through CCI and other agencies.
- Providing direct information, support, and assistance where young people are most in need.
- Dealing with crisis presentations and liaison with emergency and out of hour services.

Their statistical summary for 1998 provides clear evidence that a significant number of women come into prostitution at a young age and for some this involvement begins before they reach the age of consent.

	1996/97	**1997/98**
Total referrals	587	570
under 16s	17 (3%)	23 (4%)
16–17 year olds	76 (13%)	68 (12%)
18–20 year olds	176 (30%)	154 (27%)

Source: City Centre Initiative Statistical Summary 1998

The City Centre Initiative figures show that from a total of 570 contacts in the period between 1997 and 98, 4 per cent were young people under the age of 16. A similar rate is reflected from the previous year between 1996 and 97, where there were a total of 587 referrals of which 3 per cent were young women under the age of sixteen. When the situation of 16 to 17 year olds is considered, there is a significant increase with this age accounting for 12 per cent of the 1997 to 98 referrals and 13 per cent of the 1996 to 97 figures. These figures show that approximately 100 young women under the age of 18 were in contact with the project in both of these years.

In Dundee, figures for the number of women engaged in prostitution are difficult to come by. The main reason for this is that street work in Dundee is rare, as most women tend to work from home or in some cases from pubs within the city. Similarly, any young people who work as prostitutes are seldom seen on the streets

The Dundee Young Women's Project provides a service to young people who find themselves in prostitution. This is a unique and innovative project, which was created by the Dundee Rape Crisis Centre in 1994. The project offers a free, confidential service specifically designed for women and girls aged 18 years and under, who have been sexually abused or raped at any time. Over time, the project responded to an increase in demand from younger women involved in prostitution and in need of a supportive network.

Young people tend to end up in prostitution as a result of lack of money or lack of a place to live. There is also a strong correlation between child prostitution and running away from home or local authority care, (Wade, Biehal, Clayden and Stein, 1998). Much of this stems from experiencing sexual abuse within their homes or close family networks. The effects of abuse frequently causes serious behavioural problems, resulting in further tensions within an already dysfunctional care situation. There may also be conflict and problems with a non-abusing parent, where the young person perceives a parent as having failed to protect them. Such conflicts can contribute significantly to homelessness, as the young, sexually abused people are forced to leave the family home in order to get away from the reality, or indeed the memory, of sexual abuse. However, many young people will simply want the abuse to stop and do not want to report a close relative to the authorities which may well involve a criminal investigation. This experience is well documented in literature concerning the sexual abuse of children, (DoH, 1996).

This leaves these vulnerable young people at significant risk. Often young people will end up providing sexual services to someone who provides accommodation, money or both. Project staff talk of the need for these young people to be helped and supported, even if no formal disclosure of sexual abuse is made. One project worker, when talking of her dream for these young people said, 'what I would like to see is somewhere for these young people to go to live where they can be protected and where their wish not to disclose can be respected—the system expects too much of kids to get money, housing etc.'.

The Barnardo's publication *Whose Daughter Next?*, (Swann, 1998, pp 11–14), provides a graphic insight into how a child moves from being sexually abused by someone within the family to prostitution. This vulnerability leads to a common process that draws them into prostitution. Swann separates this process into several stages. Stage one is the ensnaring stage when a young man seeks to impress a young girl by such things as his good looks, money, maturity etc. The second stage, 'creating dependency', is when the man creates the impression that the girl cannot manage without him. Her vulnerability causes her to feel flattered and comforted. Stage three, 'taking control', is where the man begins to control where she goes, who she sees, what she wears and even in extreme cases, when she goes to the toilet. Stage four, 'total dominance', is the cumulative effect of the previous three stages, when the 'boyfriend', having become the all important person in the girl's life, has created a 'willing victim'. Simple compliance rarely satisfies him, as he also demands respect, gratitude and love.

It is important not to succumb to a gender stereotype of all prostitutes being female, and to recognise that it is not only young women who are involved in prostitution. Young men also sell sex and often find it difficult to approach and access services. Many have experienced prejudice and ignorance and have been referred to inappropriate services and often with little concern on issues of confidentiality.

In Edinburgh, the Spittal Street Centre has worked with male prostitutes for the last four years. They provide a drop-in facility, a one to one counselling service, general advice on benefits and relationships and a mobile bus one night a week to provide an on-the-spot harm reduction and information service. During 1998, they have had 37 individual contacts with male prostitutes up to the age of 30 years. In four cases the boys were under the age of 16. Around 90 per cent of these referrals have had some experience of the care system and the majority have been sexually abused. The project suspects that the potential number of young people is probably higher, as many of the boys under the age of 20 are working from home and are less visible. There has been no significant change in numbers contacting the project over the last four years, with a consistent rate of approximately 40 young men per year contacting the centre. Generally, there are very few services in Scotland that exist to target young men who sell sex. Initiatives do exist in a number of major cities, but these services often have limited resources.

Social Security Benefit Changes

Whilst a number of individual problems and issues may contribute to young homelessness and individual vulnerability, some recognition needs to be given to structural oppression and the role of the state. It could be argued that successive government policies have marginalised young people in society. One such piece of legislation is the 1988 Social Security Act.

There is no doubt that the removal of benefits to 16 and 17 year olds by this legislation had a major impact. It is arguably one of the most discriminatory and punitive pieces of legislation of recent years. Not only did it contribute to the increased vulnerability of young people, it endorsed a message of social exclusion to this age group of the population. Although the 1988 Act was the most significant factor, it was not the only policy change to affect young people. Broad, (1998: pp 88–89), has highlighted the connection between poverty and young people leaving care. He cites a series of measures that have increased poverty for young people and forced them towards clandestine routes of survival and making money.

Without exception, all the projects visited cited the cumulative social security policy changes as having a significant impact on the life style of young people. They also commented on the hidden, but equally significant effect of these policy changes, that leave young people feeling alienated and not part of society.

Poverty

Prostitution is a moneymaking activity, and this is a significant reason why some people become involved in prostitution. They may use the money to support a drug habit or to put a roof over their head, but it is the money that is worked for.

Government training programmes for young people currently pay £45 per week and the newly introduced and much publicised minimum wage of £3.60 per hour does not apply to this age group. Employers can therefore pay below this figure to 16 and 17 year olds. Projects reported that the simple fact is that money can be made as a prostitute, and £40 per session would not be uncommon for rent boys to earn. It is therefore important to recognise that a young person may often see prostitution as a short term solution to money problems, without them recognising the longer term dangers associated with what rapidly becomes a way of life.

Drug Issues

Drug misuse by prostitutes has been well documented in the literature. For some people, prostitution is the way that they get the money to support a drug habit and for others drugs are used in order to make prostitution bearable. Jeffries, (1997: p 112) reports that some prostitutes use drugs to help them cope with their feelings of self-hatred and revulsion for what they are involved in. Hoigard and Finstad, (1992), highlight the fact that some people with drug dependency problems move into prostitution to finance their drug habit.

In Edinburgh, the Spittal Street Centre reported recreational drug usage among rent boys with a lot of them using drugs on a daily basis and some intravenously. Hoigard and Finstad report that in Oslo, drug use is a central element in many prostitutes' lives. It is, they say, part of the street culture.

Drug misuse was reported by all the projects as being part of the lifestyle of the prostitutes. Both male and female prostitutes use drugs to block the bad feelings that go with being a prostitute. In Glasgow, the City Centre Initiative estimate that 70 to 95 per cent of prostitutes are intravenous drug users. This very much adds to the dangers for vulnerable young people, in view of the fact that the city has the highest drug related death toll in Scotland.

Conclusion

It is only recently that the plight of vulnerable young people leaving care has been addressed, with local authorities now having at least some legally defined powers and duties. We are also continually challenged by the child protection issues that affect children and young people in society. Child prostitution is one of those issues. There is some increasing evidence that the dangers associated with this activity and the needs of young people are being recognised and addressed. An illustration of a less punitive approach is the call to treat young prostitutes as victims and not criminals.

In Scotland, and where children are under 16, there is strong evidence to suggest that the welfare approach of the children's hearing system is the best way to meet their needs. The position of 16 and 17 year olds is less clear. One of the challenges in Scotland is to devise a system of targeting services and support in response to the vulnerability of this age group. One very radical possibility at the criminal justice/child care interface, would be referring alleged offences of 'soliciting' of 16 and 17 year olds to the welfare orientated forum of the children's hearing system. This, however, would only be a short term operational consideration change and is unlikely to be achieved in any case.

What is called for is a more radical consideration about how we view young people in society. Not only is it important to recognise the existence of child prostitution, but how it connects with other social problems such as child abuse, poverty, homelessness, drug addiction and crime. Government pledges about eradicating social exclusion requires that direct action is taken towards engaging young people. To do this, there has to be the development of research, policy, knowledge and practice wisdom towards this very vulnerable group in society.

References

Barrett, D. (1997). *Child Prostitution in the UK*. University of Luton/Children's Society.

Barrett, D. (Ed.) (1997). *Child Prostitution in Britain*. University of Luton/The Children's Society.

Basserman L. (1967). *The Oldest Profession: A History of Prostitution*. London: Arthur Barker.

BBC News, 29th January, 1998. http//news.bbc.uk

BBC Reporting Scotland, Friday, 16th January, 1999.

Braye, S. and Preston, M. (1997). *Practising Social Work Law*, (2nd Edn), pp 4546. BASW/Macmillan.

Broad, B. (1998). *Young People Leaving Care: Life After the Children Act 1989*. Jessica Kingsley.

Corby, B. (1993). *Child Abuse: Towards a Knowledge Base*. Open University Press.

Department of Health (1996). *Child Protection: Messages from Research*. HMSO.

Finklehor, D. (1986). *Child Sexual Abuse: A Sourcebook*. Sage.

Hoigard, C. and Finstad, F. (1992). *Backstreet Prostitution, Money and Love*. Cambridge: Polity Press.

Jeffries, S. (1997). *The Idea of Prostitution*. North Melbourne: Spinifex.

Kempe, R.S. and Kempe, H.C. (1978). *Child Abuse*. London: Fontana/Open Original Books.

Manson-Smith, D. (1995). *The Legal System of Scotland*. HMSO.

Scottish Office (1995). Statistical Bulletin No. SWK/CH/1995/19.

Scottish Office (1998). *Children's Safeguard Review*. Stationary Office.

Swann, S. (1998). *Who's Daughter Next? Children Abused Through Prostitution*. London: Barnardo's.

The Children (Scotland) Act, 1995, Section 52.

Tisdall, E.K.M. (1998). *The Children (Scotland) Act, 1995: Developing Policy, and Law for Scotland's Children*. Edinburgh: HMSO/Children in Scotland.

Wade, J. and Biehal, N. with Clayden, J. and Stein, M. (1998). *Going Missing: Young People Absent from Care*. Chichester: Wiley.

Chapter 10

Conclusion

David Barrett and Nicola Mullenger

Introduction

During October, 1999, the Dutch Parliament in The Hague overturned its ban on brothels in an attempt to legalise and sanitise the industry. Prostitution has never been illegal in the Netherlands—only the venue in which it occurs. Passing the ban in 1912, Calvinist campaigners sought to punish those exploiting women; the women themselves they considered victims. The tolerant Dutch turned a blind eye. Like the coffee shops where marijuana is sold, the brothels were criminal but allowed to operate in clearly defined areas. The law, which comes into effect next summer, will mean that brothels, sex clubs, private houses and windows where sex is on sale will have to have permits and meet standards set by local authorities.

Could this action by the Dutch be indicative of further such developments in wider Europe? Or, if only some countries take these actions, cross-border movements for abusive purposes can only increase, (Levy, 1999).

At the end of November, 1998, the 'First European Meeting of the Main Partners in the Fight against Child Sex Tourism' was held in Brussels in the presence of His Majesty, the King of the Belgians. Organised at the initiative of the European Commission and attended by representatives of its various departments, as well as of the other European Institutions, international organisations, national administrations, professional associations in the tourism sector and the non-governmental organisations concerned, this meeting highlighted the perceived progress made in taking action in this field over the previous two years.

At the conference, research suggested that most child prostitutes of whatever age, are actually integrated into the mainstream prostitution market serving all prostitute users, rather than working in some discrete 'market niche' that caters solely to the desires of 'paedophiles' (abusers of pre-puberty children) or abusers of other young people of teenage years. There are girls aged between 10 and 14 years of age prostituting alongside older teenagers and young women not only in the mining encampments of Latin America, the brothel districts of India and Bangladesh, and the tourist areas of the Caribbean and South East Asia, but also in the streets in red light areas in affluent Western countries. While some of their clients are paedophiles, a great many of them, probably the majority, are first and foremost prostitute users who become child sex abusers through their prostitute use, rather than the other way round, (O'Connell Davidson, 1999).

O'Connell Davidson argues that this is not because they have a focused sexual interest in children, but because they are morally and sexually indiscriminate. They do not really care whether the girl they take from a brothel or bar is 14 or 24, providing they 'fancy' the look of her. Furthermore, child sexual abuse becomes just one more sexual experience in the range that is on offer to them as 'consumers'.

However, understanding child and youth sex work requires some complex mapping. Their entry into prostitution is not always, or only, orchestrated by criminals. It is precipitated by poverty and other forms of social exclusion and it is facilitated by ordinary people in mainstream everyday society, such as some taxi drivers, hotel workers and bar owners.

Another leading proponent of the overlap that exists between the adult and youth sex market, (Jeffreys, 1999), argues that attempts to separate out the child from adult prostitution, in order to end the former whilst maintaining the latter, are fundamentally flawed. As a result of the 1989 United Nations Convention on the Rights of the Child, there has been an increasing interest in the issue of child labour and particularly child prostitution, in the 1990s. There has been considerable unanimity amongst human rights agencies and NGOs that both child prostitution and trafficking are violations of human rights and need to be eliminated. There has not been such unanimity on the prostitution and trafficking of adult women. In fact, in the last 10 years there has been some backing away from the United Nations understanding of the unacceptability of prostitution as exemplified in the 1949 Convention Against Trafficking in Persons. This retreat has centred on the notion that only some kinds of prostitution need to be considered harmful, i.e. 'forced' prostitution and 'child' prostitution. So-called 'free' prostitution is said by organisations such as Anti-Slavery International, for instance, to be legitimate work which needs to be accepted as such, (Bindman, 1998).

Feminist anti-prostitution activists and theorists such as Kathleen Barry, (1995), have demonstrated that prostitution has undergone a process of industrialisation since the 1960s. In this process, prostituted women and children have come under the control of big business in the western world as prostitution has been legalised and normalised. The trafficking of women for prostitution internationally, has become much more organised, with criminal and business networks making very serious profits from the practice, (De Stoop, 1992). An International Labour Office (ILO) Report, (Lim, 1998), supplies powerful evidence to suggest that prostitution is being organised on quite a new scale and that it has been integrated significantly into national economies in the last decade. The harmfulness of child prostitution to its victims is only different from adult prostitution to a degree. The very reasons posited in the ILO Report on why child prostitution is supposed to be particularly heinous, are precisely those forms of harm that are involved in adult prostitution too. The ILO Report specifies the great physical and psychological damage suffered by children from sexual exploitation as the basis of its distinction between child and adult prostitution. This damage is described in a 1996 ILO Report in more detail, (Lim, 1998).

In all societies, and particularly those often the destination of prostitution tourists, which retain the most severe forms of male dominance and in which women and girls have exceptionally low social status, women experience sexual abuse in childhood and adulthood which can rob them of self-esteem, independence or the chance to marry. They can be seen as less worthy of education or an economic liability. Women and girls are taught that the possibility of their sexual use is their only economic asset. They are born into societies in which a rampant demand for commercial sexual access to their persons by men, represented in the fact that they are likely to be offered money whilst just going about their daily business, marks them out as sexual objects and men out as abusers. The argument of 'choice' is used by those determined studiously to ignore these facts of the material power difference between men and women, those committed to a rampant individualism, (Jeffreys, 1999. Also Jeffreys, 1997, for further discussion on the issue of choice).

Summarising the Contributions

We saw in Chapter 2 an examination of the political, social and economic developments that have occurred since 1989, reflecting the changing faces of the different regions in Europe. Western Europe has maintained its political and economic position in the world market, despite the threat of recession and the challenge of globalisation. Both the strengthening of the EU under the Maastricht Treaty and the establishment of the single market have consolidated the power of Western Europe. CEE has not had the same success; only Poland has successfully fulfilled the economic transition and has reached the equivalent output levels that it had in 1989. Other areas, such as Kosovo, have witnessed large-scale conflict and devastation as a result of nationalistic leaders and ethnic diversity. This has undone the progress made in the fields of economic stability and general development of the region's infrastructure.

Unemployment and poverty have figured predominantly in the problems associated with CEE. Political and economic reform has taken precedent over social welfare, resulting in the deterioration of secure employment and subsidies on rent and food. Consequently, the gap between voluntary and state welfare services has been widened. One cannot deny the hardships suffered, yet, according to Brown and Shah, it is difficult to identify alternative solutions. Unemployment has also been a major problem for the countries of Western Europe. Fortunately, we have seen the establishment of better welfare systems which are able to cope more efficiently.

Despite the problems caused by the transition from communist to democratic, the ideology which dictates that capitalism, democracy and the free market is the only way forward, is, according to Brown and Shah, the solution to economic development. Indeed, they stick to Lech Walesa's sentiment that capitalism may be the worst system, except for all the others.

Lenihan and Dean in Chapter 3 examined the problem of child prostitution in England. After a series of successful campaigns by agencies in Britain, they feel that public awareness of child prostitution is now widespread. This public acknowledgement supports the voluntary organisations in their willingness to confront the issue of child prostitution that has only surfaced in the last ten years. It is essential that agencies involved in working with children in prostitution take action while the issue is still in the limelight; the problem must not be allowed to slip into the background again as it did at the end of the 19th century. Lenihan and Dean see the need for creative strategic thinking about exit routes from prostitution and the provision of a strong support network to avoid long-term emotional and physical health problems. To deal with the complex issues that child prostitution presents, any such service will require a multi-disciplinary approach.

Lenihan and Dean state that we must be wary of developments in the European Community which, in liberalising trade, will increase the risk of children becoming another commodity. Already there is evidence of prostitution as a result of the collapse of the Eastern Bloc. From research in this chapter, the authors conclude that where there are gulfs between the rich and the poor, prostitution is likely to flourish and children are likely to be involved.

Although it is important to recognise the situation concerning child prostitution abroad, we must not neglect the problem that exists in wider Britain today. The authors believe that research shows that the number of children involved in prostitution today can be measured in thousands. They are not suggesting a massive increase in the numbers involved, but what is apparent is that there are too many children involved. These children are victims of the welfare system because there are still those who deny a problem exists and, as they note, as one speaker remarked at a recent conference on children involved in prostitution, 'If there is one local authority in this country which says it does not have a problem of child prostitution, then they aren't looking closely enough'.

In Chapter 4 we saw the position in Ireland. Despite the general increase in prosperity in Ireland, poverty is still an unfortunate feature of Irish society. This is accompanied by the problem of child prostitution. The liberalisation of Irish society during recent years has allowed the problem to be identified and Brooke's work among others, has started to analyse and assess the problem.

Prostitution is not a way of life that children choose for themselves, but a consequence of a variety of reasons as identified by Brooke in *Ways into Child Prostitution*. He examines the various issues involving children at risk in the Irish society. The lack of government intervention in child-care could be argued as one of the core problems in a country which still has a child poverty level at the second highest in the European Union. Homelessness, problems within the juvenile justice system, child abuse often rooted in the Catholic Church and educational disadvantage in the working class are all, he argues, classic causes that could lead directly to child prostitution.

The knowledge of child prostitution in Ireland is limited due to the lack of empirical evidence. The definition of prostitution is still not clear. Furthermore, research is still hindered by the secrecy of any sexual activity or abuse, especially with under age people. However, he provides useful figures by Barnado's and the Eastern Health Board Working Group. The ways into child prostitution, although complex, have been similarly identified by several different bodies. All noted a similar range of factors that have influenced involvement in child prostitution including a connection between prostitution and homelessness.

In the third part of his work, Brooke looks at ways in which prostitution can be prevented and how the children already involved can be helped. Although there are the beginnings of improvements, centre-based and outreach services, there is a long way still to go. He argues that a national strategy is needed to consolidate the work of the local agencies.

Mullenger discusses Italy in Chapter 5, where she has outlined the importance of migration and social and economic poverty in the overall context of prostitution. However, youth prostitution does not rely solely upon these factors; it occurs daily in the 'sophisticated' countries of Europe. Progress is being made with the introduction, in February, 1999, of Article 18 of the new immigration law, which will help to provide both ethical and legal status for 'foreign' women and young people. Mullenger recognises that, through lack of solid identity and self-esteem, prostitutes might find it hard to seek protection and advice. For aid workers, it is essential that advice about sexually transmitted diseases, birth control and other issues, can be distributed to the sex workers.

In Italy, the link between crime and migrants is not helping the aid agencies at all; only an increased awareness of cultural and equality issues will start to resolve this problem. Better communication and longer term support networks are necessary to link the problems of Western Europe and the developing countries of the East, on this issue. The distinctions between the different origins of the sex workers should also be recognised.

For sex workers who do manage to return home, support systems must be developed to provide assistance in the complex task of re-adapting to their former life. As a sex worker, the limited opportunity to return home would mean struggling with cultural and identity issues; but staying would only maintain their position as a stateless person, with no papers, at the mercy of criminals.

In Chapter 6, consideration was given as to whether the safe sex message is still as effective in a culture of sexual openness such as that of the Netherlands. There exists a dilemma for the health educators; 'no sex' or 'safer sex'? One could argue that young people are entitled to discover their own sexuality and make a choice of 'no sex' or 'safe sex'. Others, with different religious or cultural views, may disagree and discourage young people from undertaking any sort of sexual activity. This, however, may well be a denial of part of their natural development. Due to the forces of supply and demand, the youth sex industry continues to grow in the Netherlands. The AIDS epidemic ensures that any trends in the sexual activity of the youth of today cannot be ignored. Indeed, in the Netherlands, problems have been tackled by interventionist health strategies and by introducing practices that are aimed at reducing levels of harm to the young sex workers.

In Chapter 7, youth prostitution in Romania was examined. Nistor and Soitu believe that the current situation involving juvenile prostitution is unsatisfactory and a fundamental change in outlook is required. Despite the increasing visibility of prostitution in recent years, there still does not appear to exist an official policy to protect and assist the young people involved (Romanian Save the Children, 1994). Nistor and Soitu believe that although today the problem has been identified, an indirect concern, outdated laws and even a general attitude that regards children as delinquent, still hinder any positive developments of this issue. They argue that the negative outlook towards juvenile prostitution needs to change, before any measures become reality in order to tackle this dangerous social phenomenon.

Chapter 8 examined the situation regarding prostitution in Russia. Sidorenko-Stephenson identifies the feature of urban marginality as a consequence of the transition from the Soviet Union. The reform process has started to create Russian cities that resemble those of the West where crime, homelessness and prostitution are all present. Problems are further exacerbated, especially for the young, by the lack of opportunities for legitimate employment and the absence of facilities for rehabilitation. Due to the undeveloped child care system and the severe conditions in children's institutions, according to NAN, 200,000 children run away each year from state homes.

Child refugees and migrant children, which the Federal Migration Service number at 300,000, are at risk in Russia as they are excluded from the system of social protection. Existing legislation does not allow children to be granted refugee status and they are sent back to where they came from. Children in Moscow without a residence permit are refused education and also they have no rights to health care.

There does not exist any effective system of shelter for children in Russia. NAN has established twelve shelters in Moscow and there are several small shelters run by NGOs, but without a Moscow permit, entrance is refused. Alternative shelter is at the militia reception centres which only allow residence for a limited period and often lock up the children.

There are no special organisations or provisions to assist the youth involved in prostitution. Special 'vice squads' organised by the military are understaffed and periodic campaigns against corrupt military personnel who take bribes from prostitutes are ineffective. Policing prostitution in Russia has had a corrupting impact on the police, much like the situation in the United States. The military themselves are often guilty of demanding bribes or sex from under age prostitutes.

The limited legislation that does exist, the author argues, is rather ineffective. The aim is to prevent people, especially minors, from becoming involved in prostitution. Information on 160 procurement cases is held by the Petersburg Department on the Control of Prostitution and Pornography. However, in 1995, out of 28 criminal proceedings against brothel keeping and procurement, only one was brought to court and then only a suspended sentence was handed down.

Sidorenko-Stephenson believes that while protection of children already involved in prostitution is vital, the problem can only be solved by prevention. Development of the child care system, including foster care with the aim of reducing abuse and neglect, will improve the situation and discourage children from entering prostitution. There have been signs that the situation is improving, although only an extensively developed system of support will protect children from exploitation. UNICEF and the Ministry of Labour and Social Development are conducting a joint experiment to establish regional Children's Ombudsmen, a system of foster care is being developed in Samara, adoption centres have been created in fifteen regions of Russia and a number of NGOs have created shelters and day centres for street children.

The policies involving prostitution are still a cause for debate between the 'liberals' and the 'radicals'. The former argue that the introduction of criminal punishment cannot be effective and encourage economic measures and the improvement of education. The latter want to legalise prostitution and make prostitutes pay taxes and receive medical help. In Moscow the authorities have even considered creating zones of tolerance where prostitution can take place, although there have been problems in trying to execute this plan.

Certain people still believe that prostitution deserves criminal punishment. Their claims of 'sexual de-moralisation' have been supported by the new 'pro-life' movement, the nationalist and the conservative political camps. A victory was won recently, with the support of the State Duma Committee on Family, Women and Youth, over the Ministry of Health and the Ministry of Education, that disallowed the introduction of sex education into schools. Furthermore, a network of family planning clinics are currently deprived of state funding due to the opposition in the State Duma.

The transition has increased the risk of child exploitation in the field of prostitution. The situation demands immediate short term solutions to protect those already involved and a long term strategy to prevent the growth of this dangerous occupation.

Chapter 9 looked at child prostitution in Scotland today. The issue has only recently been recognised and addressed as a problem. However, we are now starting to see new legislation to protect those caught up in prostitution as well as accepting the calls for young prostitutes to be treated as victims and not criminals.

Buckley and Brodie believe there is strong evidence to suggest that the Children's Hearing System is the best approach to dealing with children under 16 involved in prostitution. They still believe though that a new system must be devised to provide services and support to deal with the vulnerability of this age group. One radical suggestion they put forward is the possibility of referring alleged offences of 'soliciting' by 16 and 17 year olds to the welfare orientated forum of the Children's Hearing System.

Above all, the chapter recognises the need to change the perception of children in Scottish society. The government must tackle social problems such as child abuse, poverty, homelessness, drug addiction and crime and only then will there be a realistic hope of reducing child prostitution. Research into this vulnerable section of society must continue, so that knowledge of the subject can assist in strategic policy making to reduce the problem.

Some Further Reflections

So what can we conclude from these contributions from around Europe? The economic and political changes and their subsequent influences and effects are analysed thoroughly by Brown and Shah and are developed further in most chapters, such as Romania and Ireland. But these are only some of the issues in what is becoming a seemingly more entangled web of inter-relating factors. Below we outline some of the key factors that have emerged from this collection of material.

Migration and sex work in Europe

In the last ten years, the number of women from the developing world in the European prostitution market has become a social fact, with a stable and structural character. The first migrant women arrived in the early 1970s, particularly in Northern and Western Europe, spreading to Southern Europe slightly later. In general, the movement of 'export and import' is in the hands of international criminal organisations, or individual intermediaries which appear to offer legitimate opportunities but are underpinned by criminal pressures. Some of these women may have been lured into prostitution under false pretences. Some may start sex work whilst waiting for political asylum (e.g. Belgium, Germany). Others, however, analysed the options available to them in their own countries and decided to earn their living as migrant sex workers in Europe. Such women are vulnerable and often unfamiliar with the appropriate language and society. The illegal nature of their migration and work means that their status is precarious, which makes estimates of their numbers difficult. As a result of their situation, migrant prostitutes tend to work in the sections of their market where earnings are relatively low and potential dependency on third persons is greatest. Although the majority of this group is evidently female, it also applies to males too.

Health matters—a lot!

Evidence from Europe demonstrates that women sex workers, in general, are not currently experiencing high levels of HIV infection, although they may experience high levels of other STDs, (Warwick and Whitty, 1994). Many sex workers were already using condoms to prevent STDs, before the advent of HIV infection; with increasing awareness about HIV/AIDS, condom use has increased still further. In European cities such as Barcelona, Frankfurt and Milan, where HIV rates are significant among sex workers, the main risk factor is the sharing of injecting equipment.

Sex workers themselves are at risk from clients refusing to use condoms. Many women sex workers may also prefer not to use condoms with lovers or husbands, as a way of distinguishing between work and their private life. Ignorance and prejudice about the realities of sex work, on the part of officials and the general public, means that prevention campaigns often do not take account of these factors.

Let us look at two examples, firstly France. Educational workers from one of the largest organisations in Paris have the following opinion about education for young gay men: 'You can say that the gay community understood the threat of HIV and AIDS. The question today is; is the young gay generation still applying safer sex practices?' It is very hard for the government to do general campaigns on the one hand and targeted campaigns on the other. So, as far as local campaigns for gay people in France are concerned, they do occur in saunas, clubs, and bars, and there are brochures, pamphlets, safe sex equipment and condoms. However, there is a need for a stronger targeted campaign for each group who needs information. This implies that the government has to take the courage to speak about words like fuck, suck, etc. If you compare the gay community with an iceberg, then the top of the iceberg is formed by only the people who have come out, and who can say: 'We are gay, we need prevention, we want to prevent AIDS like everyone else, we are fed up with seeing our friends dying'.

The second example is from Spain. There, like in other Latin countries, homosexuality has not (yet) been accepted by the general public, as it is in Northern Europe. As a result of this, there are less public meeting places in which educators can access the gay population and, furthermore, in politics, gay issues are not on the agenda at all. A clear example of this is the low number of organisations specifically involved in providing information for young gays. One example is a non-governmental organisation in Madrid, where two staff members are doing all the work, from setting up programmes, to educating the people personally, in the entire city. The attitude and behaviour towards minorities, such as young gays, is that being gay is a matter of choice, and HIV exposure is a consequence, brought upon themselves. This was reflected in educational programmes in general and was felt by the second generation. In Spain, there is no infrastructure and awareness of reaching young gay people historically, nor will there be in the near future. Historically, homosexuals were not the group most highly exposed to HIV, thus the government, in its educational campaigns, focused on the explosive exposure in the intravenous drug users (IVDU) population, (The French and Spanish examples are both from van Steijn and Milbauer, 1995).

Differences and denial

From the descriptions of the various countries, it will be obvious that there are striking differences between the southern and the northern countries of Europe, regarding the awareness of the second generation of gay men. This is reflected in the policy, education (including training for educators), budgeting, social research and the establishment of official organisations. Another difference is the degree of responsibility men take for their actions. Adult women are seen as responsible for their abuse in prostitution either as unharmed or choosing to be harmed, whilst children are seen to be off limits for some. In fact, men's prostitution abuse is not 'natural' behaviour, but the result of the idea, some argue, that such sexual abuse of women and children is vital for health, enjoyed by women and a right of manhood. The abuse of power is relevant to young men too.

Education and employment opportunities

There appears to be a relationship between having an advanced education system, with the consequent employment opportunities, and the numbers of indigenous young people involved in sex work. In these more advanced countries, like the Netherlands, we see migrant and other trafficked young people but only a very small proportion of locals. In others, like Romania and Russia, the indications are less hopeful for even the local young people.

In some countries there is now a greater understanding in society in general about young people's involvement in sex work. In England, there has been a shift towards viewing the young people as victims of abuse, and thus needing help from the welfare system rather than being subjected to the punitive justice system. The abusers and exploiters are also more likely to come to the attention of the criminal justice system now.

The lack of education and employment opportunities for young people in their own countries, normally based on economic conditions at a national level, are some of the factors that create the 'right' conditions for young people to be involved in the sex industry; Brooke has given these conditions some attention in the Irish chapter.

Increasing inequalities

Easier cross-border movement, political unrest in South-east Europe, the growth of international crime and increasing economic inequalities all paint a gloomy scenario for the young sex worker in Europe at the beginning of a new century. Conditions are 'right' (i.e. generally worsening) for their business to flourish and are likely to continue to be so, with little sign that these factors will improve. Therefore, in the short term, legitimate opportunities in a modern Europe are likely to be few and far between, especially if you are from a poorer country or from a poorer background.

With changing migration patterns and the increasing numbers of refugees from the various war zones our responses to the needs of young people appear to be reactive, poorly resourced and uncoordinated. The fragmentation of Europe and its youth is taking place with some polarised positions emerging. It is rather simplistic, however, to say that the peoples of the rich countries simply exploit and abuse members of the poorer countries. The market dynamics are more sophisticated; there are internal as well as external forces at work.

New models

Amongst the contributions, various models and approaches can be identified as 'good practice', but if we try to transfer such models from one country to another these attempts need to be undertaken with great care, local contexts and conditions are important to recognise. However, there is much good practice to be shared in the context of community safety. The fundamental question is '*why is the phenomenon of youth sex work taking hold?*' We might adopt a conservative, liberal, radical or child centred approach, but all of them offer some advantages and disadvantages. A highly punitive regime might lead to people fleeing to other locations, whereas a liberal regime often means that a particular location becomes a sex centre for abusers and the abused alike.

'Wish lists' for change also have to be treated with caution. The European Commission may publish and support such lists (e.g. Beddoe, 1999: p 200), but is the Commission really putting its 'money where its mouth is'? We think there is a paucity of empirical evidence in the EC's favoour.

It is often argued 'more evidence is needed before we can take any action'. This is a simple delaying and paralysing tactic—usually most effective! In this book evidence of young prostitutes, in a variety of forms, and some being trafficked, is plentiful. Reform, behavioural change, resources—yes, of course they are all required, but if there is ever a case for political leadership for change, this is it. Or otherwise 'What price our children?' in the EC remains a legitimate and real question. Punters ask the question of our children regularly—What's the price? How much? and agree to pay more for unprotected sex and more for the lower age of the child. Our children need to be unfettered from such conditions.

The evidence from this book suggests that although much progress has been made in understanding young people and sex work with advances in education, harm reduction, exit strategies etc., there is no sign of the numbers involved 'in the business' reducing. On the contrary! A gloomy message indeed which must be addressed by those at the highest level.

References

Barry, K. (1995). *The Prostitution Sexuality.* New York: NYU Press.

Beddoe, C. (1999). In *First European Meeting of the Main Partners in the Fight Against Child Sex Tourism* (24/5 Nov 1998, Brussels), p 200. Brussels: EC.

Bindman, J. (1998). An International Perspective on Slavery in the Sex Industry. In Kempadoo, K. and Doezema, J. (Eds.). *Global Sex Workers.* New York: Routledge.

De Stoop, C. (1992). *They are so Sweet, Sir.* Leuven: Limitless Asia.

Jeffreys, S. (1997). *The Idea of Prostitution.* Melbourne: Spinifex.

Jeffreys, S. (1999). Child Verses Adult Prostitution: A False Distinction. In *First European Meeting of the Main Partners in the Fight Against Child Sex Tourism* (24/5 Nov 1998, Brussels). Brussels: EC.

Levy, A. (1999). Cross Border Movement for Abusive Purposes: The Adequacy of UK Safeguards. *ChildRight,* No. 159: pp 6–8.

Lim, L.L. (Ed.) (1998). *The Sex Sector.* Geneva: International Labour Office.

O'Connell Davidson, J. (1999). In *First European Meeting of the Main Partners in the Fight Against Child Sex Tourism* (24/5 Nov 1998, Brussels), p 25. Brussels: EC.

van Steijn, P. and Milbauer, D. (1995). HIV/AIDS Education for Young Gay Men: A European Profile. In Reinders, J. and Vermeer, V. (Eds.). *How to Reach Youth in the Outside School Setting.* Woerden, Netherlands: NIGZ.

Warwick, I. and Whitty, G. (1994). *When it Matters: Developing HIV/AIDS Education with Young Homeless People.* London: HES.

In Waiting:
Night and Day

Nicola Mullinger

The notion of 'waiting' comes from the legal and punitive system which denies
the proper rights for working in this profession and the complicated political
issues associated with the registration of such people. It extends to the painful
existence of waiting for: punter/client and pimp/racketeer in hazardous conditions during the 'night'. Furthermore during the 'day' there is 'enabling
time' to heal, learn new skills and receive legal documents. 'Night' came about
in the winter of 1997 and 'day' in the summer of 1999, with different young
women in Padova, Italy.

> *It's not a matter of prevention of migration or prostitution, but prevention
> of all kinds of situations where women can become dependant."*
>
> (Lucia Brussa, TAMPEP Final Report 1996,
> section Western Europe, p 259, Amsterdam.)

All photographs were taken with the knowledge of the women concerned.
Identities were specifically avoided. I wanted to highlight the stigma attached
to being a working woman, and its associated prejudice. As no-one knows
what a young exploited sex worker looks like, faces are not needed in the
photographs. Moreover, in contemporary society the choice to work in the
sex industry is often not a personal one. This is the case for most of the women
depicted, who are predominantly from Albania. Indeed, it is work that can
supplement family income or fuel addictions, and is often commenced by the
proximity of unavoidable external influences.

Copyright of Photographs and Text: Nicola Mullenger

Acknowledgements

I would like to thank Mimosa for their ongoing work and belief in this project, especially Diega Carraretto, Elisa Bedim and all the women involved. Foundazione Italiana per la Fotografia, for the materials to produce 'Night' and Southern Arts for the financial support of the residency for 'Day'. To all the individuals who helped along the way: including Pier Paolo Cariglia for translations, Lynne Ravenscroft, Lorenza Orlando for access to further research, Jose Machado Pais and Ricardo Pais Mamede for their time and Pavia Fotografia, Paul Mellor and Gareth Young for enthusiasm. To all the associations who tirelessly answered my requests including On the Road, Comiato per i Diritti Civili delle Prostitute and Anti Slavery International (UK) for the use of their library. With thanks to Liz and Roger.

This work is dedicated to those out there struggling.

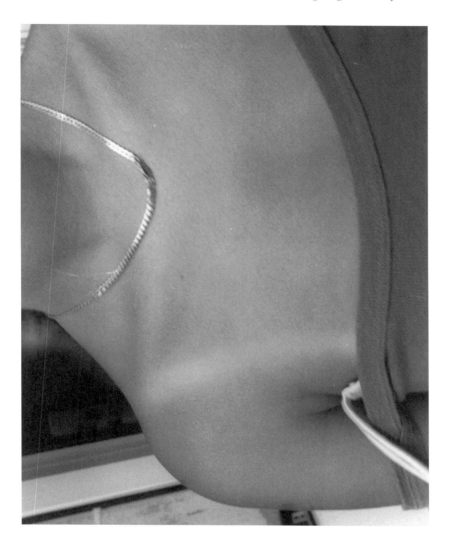

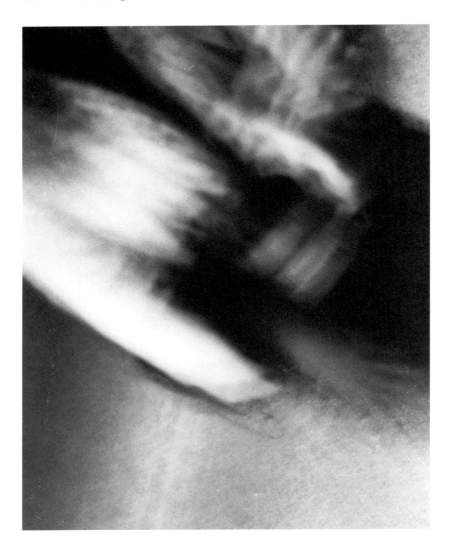